Charles Sumner

Expulsion of the President

Charles Sumner

Expulsion of the President

ISBN/EAN: 9783337402082

Printed in Europe, USA, Canada, Australia, Japan

Cover: Foto ©ninafisch / pixelio.de

More available books at **www.hansebooks.com**

EXPULSION OF THE PRESIDENT.

OPINION

OF

HON. CHARLES SUMNER, OF MASSACHUSETTS,

IN THE CASE OF THE

IMPEACHMENT OF ANDREW JOHNSON,

PRESIDENT OF THE UNITED STATES.

WASHINGTON:
GOVERNMENT PRINTING OFFICE.
1868.

OPINION

OF

HON. CHARLES SUMNER, OF MASSACHUSETTS.

IN THE CASE OF THE

IMPEACHMENT OF ANDREW JOHNSON,

PRESIDENT OF THE UNITED STATES.

I voted against the rule of the Senate allowing Opinions to be filed in this proceeding, and regretted its adoption. With some hesitation I now take advantage of the opportunity, if not the invitation, which it affords. Voting "guilty" on all the articles, I feel that there is no need of explanation or apology. Such a vote is its own best defender. But I follow the example of others.

BATTLE WITH SLAVERY.

This is one of the last great battles with slavery. Driven from these legislative chambers, driven from the field of war, this monstrous power has found a refuge in the Executive Mansion, where, in utter disregard of the Constitution and laws, it seeks to exercise its ancient far-reaching sway. All this is very plain. Nobody can question it. Andrew Johnson is the impersonation of the tyrannical slave power. In him it lives again. He is the lineal successor of John C. Calhoun and Jefferson Davis; and he gathers about him the same supporters. Original partisans of slavery north and south; habitual compromisers of great principles; maligners of the Declaration of Independence; politicians without heart; lawyers, for whom a technicality is everything, and a promiscuous company who at every stage of the battle have set their faces against equal rights; these are his allies. It is the old troop of slavery, with a few recruits, ready as of old for violence—cunning in device, and heartless in quibble. With the President at their head, they are now entrenched in the Executive Mansion.

Not to dislodge them is to leave the country a prey to one of the most hateful tyrannies of history. Especially is it to surrender the Unionists of the rebel States to violence and bloodshed. Not a month, not a week, not a day should be lost. *The safety of the Republic requires action at once.* The lives of innocent men must be rescued from sacrifice.

I would not in this judgment depart from that moderation which belongs to the occasion; but God forbid that, when called to deal with so great an offender, I should affect a coldness which I cannot feel. Slavery has been our worst enemy, assailing all, murdering our children, filling our homes with mourning, and darkening the land with tragedy; and now it rears its crest anew, with Andrew Johnson as its representative. Through him it assumes once more to rule the Republic and to impose its cruel law. The enormity of his conduct is aggravated by his barefaced treachery. He once declared himself the Moses of the

4

colored race Behold him now the Pharaoh. With such treachery in such a
cause there can be no parley. Every sentiment, every conviction, every vow
against slavery must now be directed against him. Pharaoh is at the bar of
the Senate for judgment.

The formal accusation is founded on certain recent transgressions, enumerated
in articles of impeachment, but it is wrong to suppose that this is the whole
case. It is very wrong to try this impeachment merely on these articles. It
is unpardonable to higgle over words and phrases when, for more than two
years the tyrannical pretensions of this offender, now in evidence before the
Senate, as I shall show, have been manifest in their terrible, heart-rending consequences.

IMPEACHMENT A POLITICAL AND NOT A JUDICIAL PROCEEDING.

Before entering upon the consideration of the formal accusation, instituted by
the House of Representatives of the United States in their own name and in the
name of all of the people thereof, it is important to understand the nature of the
proceeding; and here on the threshold we encounter the effort of the apologists
who have sought in every way to confound this great constitutional trial with
an ordinary case at Nisi Prius and to win for the criminal President an Old
Bailey acquittal, where on some quibble the prisoner is allowed to go without
day. From beginning to end this has been painfully apparent, thus degrading
the trial and baffling justice. Point by point has been pressed, sometimes by
counsel and sometimes even by senators, leaving the substantial merits un-
touched, as if on a solemn occasion like this, involving the safety of the Republic,
there could be any other question.

The first effort was to call the Senate, sitting for the trial of impeachment, a
court, and not a Senate. Ordinarily names are of little consequence, but it cannot
be doubted that this appellation has been made the starting-point for those technicalities which are so proverbial in courts. Constantly we have been reminded
of what is called our judicial character and of the supplementary oath we have
taken, as if a senator were not always under oath, and as if other things within
the sphere of his duties were not equally judicial in character. Out of this
plausible assumption has come that fine-spun thread which lawyers know so well
how to weave.

The whole mystification disappears when we look at our Constitution, which
in no way speaks of impeachment as judicial in character, and in no way speaks
of the Senate as a court. On the contrary it uses positive language, inconsistent
with this assumption and all its pretended consequences. On this head there
can be no doubt.

By the Constitution it is expressly provided that "the *judicial power* shall be
vested in one Supreme Court and in such inferior courts as the Congress may
from time to time ordain and establish," thus positively excluding the Senate
from any exercise of "the judicial power." And yet this same Constitution
provides that "the Senate shall have the sole power to try all impeachments."
In the face of these plain texts it is impossible not to conclude that in trying
impeachments senators exercise a function which is not regarded by the Constitution as "judicial," or, in other words, as subject to the ordinary conditions of
judicial power. Call it senatorial or political, it is a power by itself and subject
to its own conditions.

Nor can any adverse conclusion be drawn from the unauthorized designation
of court, which has been foisted into our proceedings. This term is very
expansive and sometimes very insignificant. In Europe it means the household
of a prince. In Massachusetts it is still applied to the legislature of the State,
which is known as the General Court. If applied to the Senate it must be interpreted by the Constitution, and cannot be made in any respect a source of power
or a constraint.

It is difficult to understand how this term, which plays such a part in present pretensions, obtained its vogue. It does not appear in English impeachments, although there is reason for it there, which is not found here. From ancient times Parliament, including both houses, has been called a court, and the House of Lords is known as a court of appeal. The judgment on English impeachments embraces not merely removal from office, as under our Constitution, but also punishment. And yet it does not appear that the lords sitting on impeachments are called a court. They are not so called in any of the cases, from the first in 1330, entitled simply, "Impeachment of Roger Mortimer, Earl of March, for Treason," down to the last in 1806, entitled, " Trial of Right Honorable Henry Lord Viscount Melville before the Lords House of Parliament in Westminster for High Crimes and Misdemeanors whereof he was accused in certain articles of Impeachment." In the historic case of Lord Bacon, we find, at the first stage, this title, "Proceedings in Parliament against Francis Bacon Lord Verulam ;" and after the impeachment was presented, the simple title, " Proceedings in the House of Lords." Had this simplicity been followed in our proceedings, one source of misunderstanding would have been removed.

There is another provision of the Constitution which testifies still further, and, if possible, more completely. It is the limitation of the judgment in cases of impeachment, making it political and nothing else. It is not in the nature of *punishment*, but in the nature of *protection to the Republic*. It is confined to removal from office and disqualification ; but, as if aware that this was no punishment, the Constitution further provides that this judgment shall be no impediment to indictment, trial, judgment, and punishment "according to law." Thus again is the distinction declared between an impeachment and a proceeding "according to law." The first, which is political, belongs to the Senate, which is a political body ; the latter, which is judicial, belongs to the courts, which are judicial bodies. The Senate removes from office; the courts punish. I am not alone in drawing this distinction. It is well known to all who have studied the subject. Early in our history it was put forth by the distinguished Mr. Bayard, of Delaware, the father of senators, in the case of Blount, and it is adopted by no less an authority than our highest commentator, Judge Story, who was as much disposed as anybody to amplify the judicial power. In speaking of this text, he says that impeachment "is not so much designed to punish the offender as *to secure the State against gross official misdemeanors ; that it touches neither his person nor his property, but simply divests him of his political capacity.* (Story, Commentaries, vol. 1, sec. 803.) All this seems to have been forgotten by certain apologists on the present trial, who, assuming that impeachment was a proceeding "according to law," have treated the Senate to the technicalities of the law, to say nothing of the law's delay.

As we discern the true character of impeachment under our Constitution we shall be constrained to confess that it is a political proceeding before a political body, with political purposes ; that it is founded on political offences, proper for the consideration of a political body and subject to a political judgment only. Even in cases of treason and bribery the judgment is political, and nothing more. If I were to sum up in one word the object of impeachment under our Constitution, meaning that which it has especially in view, and to which it is practically limited, I should say *Expulsion from Office*. The present question is, shall Andrew Johnson, on the case before the Senate, be expelled from office.

Expulsion from office is not unknown to our proceedings. By the Constitution a senator may be expelled with "the concurrence of two-thirds ;" precisely as a President may be expelled with "the concurrence of two-thirds." In each of these cases the same exceptional vote of two-thirds is required. Do not the two illustrate each other? From the nature of things they are essentially similar in character, except that on the expulsion of the President the motion is made by the House of Representatives at the bar of the Senate, while on the expulsion of a senator the motion is made by a senator. And how can we require a technicality of proceeding in the one which is rejected in the other? If the Senate is a court, bound to judicial forms on the expulsion of the President, must it not be the same on the expulsion of a senator? But nobody attributes to it any such strictness in the latter case. Numerous precedents attest how, in dealing with its own members, the Senate has sought to do substantial justice without reference to forms. In the case of Blount, which is the first in our history, the expulsion was on the report of a committee, declaring him "guilty of a high misdemeanor, entirely inconsistent with his public trust and duty as a senator." (*Annals of Congress*, 15th Congress, 1797, *p*. 44.) At least one senator has been expelled on simple motion, even without reference to a committee. Others have been expelled without any formal allegations or formal proofs.

There is another provision of the Constitution which overrides both cases. It is this : "Each house may determine its rules of proceeding." The Senate on the expulsion of its own members has already done this practically and set an example of simplicity. But it has the same power over its "rules of proceeding " on the expulsion of the President ; and there can be no reason for simplicity in the one case not equally applicable in the other. Technicality is as little consonant with the one as with the other. Each has for its object the *Public Safety*. For this the senator is expelled ; for this, also, the President is expelled. *Salus populi suprema lex*. The proceedings in each case must be in subordination to this rule.

There is one formal difference, under the Constitution, between the power to expel a senator and the power to expel the President. The power to expel a senator is unlimited in its terms. The Senate may, "with the concurrence of two-thirds, expel a member," nothing being said of the offence; whereas the President can be expelled only "for treason, bribery, or *other high crimes and misdemeanors*." A careful inquiry will show that, under the latter words, there is such a latitude as to leave little difference between the two cases. This brings us to the question of impeachable offences.

POLITICAL OFFENCES ARE IMPEACHABLE OFFENCES.

So much depends on the right understanding of the character of this proceeding, that even at the risk of protracting this discussion, I cannot hesitate to consider this branch of the subject, although what I have already said may render it superfluous. *What are impeachable offences* has been much considered in this trial, and sometimes with very little appreciation of the question. Next to the mystification from calling the Senate a court has been that other mystification from not calling the transgressions of Andrew Johnson impeachable offences.

It is sometimes boldly argued that there can be no impeachment under the Constitution of the United States, unless for an offence defined and made indictable by an act of Congress ; and, therefore, Andrew Johnson must go free, unless it can be shown that he is such an offender. But this argument mistakes the Constitution, and also mistakes the whole theory of impeachment.

It mistakes the Constitution in attributing to it any such absurd limitation. The argument is this : Because in the Constitution of the United States there are no common-law crimes, therefore there are no such crimes on which an impeachment can be maintained. To this there are two answers on the present occasion ; first, that the District of Columbia, where the President resides and exercises his functions, was once a part of Maryland, where the common law prevailed ; that when it came under the jurisdiction of the United States it brought with it the whole body of the law of Maryland, including the common law, and that at this day the common law of crimes is still recognized here. But the second answer is stronger still. By the Constitution *Expulsion from Office* is "on impeachment for and conviction of treason, bribery, *or other high crimes and misdemeanors;*" and this, according to another clause of the Constitution, is "the supreme law of the land." Now, when a constitutional provision can be executed without superadded legislation, it is absurd to suppose that such superadded legislation is necessary. Here the provision executes itself without any re-enactment; and, as for the definition of "treason" and "bribery" we resort to the common law, so for the definition of "high crimes and misdemeanors" we resort to the parliamentary law and the instances of impeachment by which it is illustrated. And thus clearly the whole testimony of English history enters into this case with its authoritative law. From the earliest text-writer on this subject (*Woodeson, Lectures, vol.* II, *p.* 601) we learn the undefined and expansive character of these offences; and these instances are in point now. Thus, where a lord chancellor has been thought to put the great seal to an ignominious treaty; a lord admiral to neglect the safeguard of the seas; an ambassador to betray his trust; a privy councillor to propound dishonorable measures; a confidential adviser to obtain exorbitant grants or incompatible employments, or *where any magistrate has attempted to subvert the fundamental law or introduce arbitary power ;* all these are high crimes and misdemeanors, according to these precedents by which our Constitution must be interpreted. How completely they cover the charges against Andrew Johnson, whether in the formal accusation or in the long antecedent transgressions to which I shall soon call attention as an essential part of the case nobody can question.

Broad as this definition may seem, it is in harmony with the declared opinions of the best minds that have been turned in this direction. Of these none so great as Edmund Burke, who, as manager on the impeachment of Warren Hastings, excited the admiration of all by the varied stores of knowledge and philosophy, illumined by the rarest eloquence, with which he elucidated his cause. These are his words :

It is by this tribunal that statesmen who abuse their power are tried before statesmen and by statesmen, *upon solid principles of state morality. It is here that those who by an abuse of power have polluted the spirit of all laws can never hope for the least protection from any of its forms.* It is here that those who have refused to conform themselves to the protection of law can never hope to escape through any of its defects. (*Bond, Speeches on Trial of Hastings, vol.* 1 *p.* 4.)

The value of this testimony is not diminished, because the orator spoke as a manager. By a professional license an advocate may state opinions which are not his own ; but a manager cannot. Representing the House of Representatives and all the people, he speaks with the responsibility of a judge, so that his words may be cited hereafter. In saying this I but follow the claim of Mr. Fox. Therefore, the words of Burke are as authoritative as beautiful.

In different but most sententious terms, Mr. Hallam, who is so great a light in constitutional history, thus exhibits the latitude of impeachment and its comprehensive grasp :

A minister is answerable for *the justice, the honesty, the utility, of all measures* emanating from the Crown, *as well as their legality;* and thus the executive administration is or *ought to be subordinate in all great matters of policy* to the superintendence and virtual control of the two houses of Parliament. (*Hallam, Constitutional History,* vol. 2, chap. 12.)

Thus, according to Hallam, even a failure in justice, honesty, and utility, as well as in legality, may be the ground of impeachment ; and the administration should in all great matters of policy be subject to the two houses of Parliament— the House of Commons to impeach and the House of Lords to try. Here again the case of Andrew Johnson is provided for.

Our best American lights are similar in character, beginning with the Federalist itself. According to this authority impeachment is for "those offences which proceed from the *misconduct of public men,* or, in other words, from the abuse or violation of some public trust; and they may with peculiar propriety be deemed *political,* as they relate to injuries done immediately to society itself."

8

(No. 65.) If ever injuries were done immediately to society itself; if ever there was an abuse or violation of public trust; if ever there was misconduct of a public man; all these are now before us in the case of Andrew Johnson. The Federalist has been echoed ever since by all who have spoken with knowledge and without prejudice. First came the respected commentator, Rawle, who specifies among causes of impeachment "the fondness for the individual extension of power;" "the influence of party and prejudice;" "the seductions of foreign states;" "the baser appetite for illegitimate emolument;" and "the involutions and varieties of vice too many and too artful to be anticipated by positive law;" all resulting in what the commentator says are "not inaptly termed *political offences.*" (Page 19.) And thus Rawle unites with the Federalist in stamping upon impeachable offences the epithet "political." If in the present case there has been on the part of Andrew Johnson no base appetite for illegitimate emolument and no yielding to foreign seductions, there has been most notoriously the influence of party and prejudice, also to an unprecedent degree an individual extension of power, and an involution and variety of vice impossible to be anticipated by positive law, all of which, in gross or in detail, is impeachable. Here it is in gross. Then comes Story, who, writing with the combined testimony of English and American history before him, and moved only by a desire of truth, records his opinion with all the original emphasis of the Federalist. His words are like a judgment. According to him the process of impeachment is intended to reach "personal misconduct, or gross neglect, or usurpation or habitual disregard of the public interests in the discharge of the duties of *political office;*" and the commentator adds that it is "to be exercised over offences committed by public men in violation of their public trust and duties;" that "the offences to which it is ordinarily applied are of a *political* character;" and that strictly speaking "the power partakes of a *political* character." (*Story's Commentaries, vol.* 2, § 746, 764.) Every word here is like an ægis for the present case. The later commentator, Curtis, is, if possible, more explicit even than Story. According to him an "impeachment is not necessarily a trial for crime;" "its purposes lie wholly beyond the penalties of the statute or customary law;" and this commentator does not hesitate to say that it is a "proceeding to ascertain *whether cause exists for removing a public officer from office;*" and he adds that "such cause of removal may exist where no offence against public law has been committed, as, where the individual has, from immorality or imbecility, *or maladministration, become unfit to exercise the office.*" (*Curtis on the Constitution, p.* 360.) Here again the power of the Senate over Andrew Johnson is vindicated, so as to make all doubt or question absurd.

I close this question of impeachable offences by asking you to consider that all the cases which have occurred in our history are in conformity with the rule which so many commentators have announced. The several trials of Pickering, Chase, Peck, and Humphreys exhibit its latitude in different forms. Official misconduct, including in the cases of Chase and Humphreys offensive utterances, constituted the high crimes and misdemeanors for which they were respectively arraigned. These are precedents. Add still further, that Madison, in debate on the appointing power, at the very beginning of our government, said: "I contend that the *wanton removal of meritorious officers* would subject the President to impeachment and removal from his own high trust." (*Elliot's Debates, vol.* 4. p. 141.) But Andrew Johnson, standing before a crowd, said of meritorious officers that "he would kick them out," and forthwith proceeded to execute his foul-mouthed menace. How small was all that Madison imagined; how small was all that was spread out in the successive impeachments of our history, if gathered into one case, compared with the terrible mass now before us.

From all these concurring authorities, English and American, it is plain that impeachment is a power broad as the Constitution itself, and applicable to the

President, Vice President, and all civil officers through whom the republic suffers or is in any way imperilled. Show me an act of evil example or influence committed by a President, and I show you an impeachable offence, which becomes great in proportion to the scale on which it is done, and the consequences which are menaced. The Republic must receive no detriment; and impeachment is one of the powers of the Constitution by which this sovereign rule is maintained.

UNTECHNICAL FORM OF PROCEDURE.

The *Form of Procedure* is a topic germane to the last head, and helping to illustrate it. Already it has been noticed in considering the political character of impeachment; but it deserves further treatment by itself. Here we meet the same latitude. It is natural that the trial of political offences, before a political body, with a political judgment only, should have less of form than a trial at common law; and yet this obvious distinction is constantly disregarded. The authorities, whether English or American, do not leave this question open to doubt.

An impeachment is not a technical proceeding, as at *nisi prius* or in a county court, where the rigid rules of the common law prevail. On the contrary, it is a proceeding according to parliamentary law, with rules of its own, unknown in ordinary courts. The formal statement and reduplication of words, which constitute the stock-in-trade of so many lawyers, are exchanged for a broader manner more consistent with the transactions of actual life. The precision of history is enough without the technical precision of an indictment. In declaring this rule I but follow a memorable judgment in a case which occupied the attention of England at the beginning of the last century. I refer to the case of the preacher Sacheverell, impeached of high crimes and misdemeanors on account of two sermons, in which he put forth the doctrine of non-resistance, and denounced the revolution of 1688, by which English liberty was saved. After the arguments on both sides, the judges on questions from the Lords answered that by the law of England and constant practice "the particular words supposed to be criminal ought to be specified in indictments." And yet, in face of this declaration by the judges of England of a familiar and indisputable rule of the common law, we have the rule of parliamentary law, which was thus set forth:

It is resolved by the lords spiritual and temporal in Parliament assembled, That by the law and usage of Parliament in prosecutions by impeachments for high crimes and misdemeanors by writing or speaking, *the particular words supposed to be criminal are not necessary to be expressly specified in such impeachments.* (*Howell's State Trials*, vol. 15, p. 467.)

The judgment here does not extend in terms beyond the case in hand; but plainly the principle announced is that in impeachments the technicalities of the common law are out of place, and the proceedings are substantially according to the rule of reason. A mere technicality, much more a quibble, such as is often so efficacious on a demurrer, is a wretched anachronism when we are considering a question of history or political duty. Even if tolerated on the impeachment of an inferior functionary, such a resort must be disclaimed on the trial of a Chief Magistrate, involving the Public Safety.

The technicalities of the law were made for protection against power, not for the immunity of a usurper or a tyrant. They are respectable when set up for the safeguard of the weak, but they are out of place on impeachments. Here again I cite Edmund Burke:

God forbid that those who cannot defend themselves upon their merits and their actions may defend themselves behind those fences and intrenchments that are made to secure the liberty of the people; that power and the abuses of power should cover themselves by those things which were made to secure liberty. (*Bond's Trial of Hastings*, vol. 1, p. 10.)

Never was there a case where this principle, belonging to the law of impeachment, was more applicable than now.

The origin of impeachment in our own Constitution and contemporary authority vindicate this very latitude. One of the apologists sought to sustain himself in an argument against this latitude, by insisting that it was with much hesitation, and only at the last moment, that this jurisdiction over impeachment was originally conferred on the Senate. This is a mistake, as will appear from a simple statement. The proposition to confer this jurisdiction on the Supreme Court was made before it had been determined that the judges should be appointed by the President with the advice and consent of the Senate. The latter conclusion was reached by a unanimous vote of the convention 7th September, 1787. On the next day, 8th September, Roger Sherman raised the objection, that the Supreme Court was "improper to try the President because the judges would be appointed by him." This objection prevailed, and the trial was at once intrusted to the Senate, by the vote of all the States with one exception; and then immediately thereafter, on the same day, the scope of impeachment was extended from "treason to bribery," so as to embrace "other high crimes and misdemeanors," and, thus intrusted and thus enlarged, it was made to embrace "the Vice-President and other civil officers of the United States."

From this simple narrative it appears, that, while the Supreme Court, *a judicial body*, was contemplated for the trial of impeachments, the jurisdiction was restrained to two well-known crimes at common law, which have since been defined by statutes of the United States; but this jurisdiction, when confided to the Senate, *a political body*, was extended to political offences, in the trial of which a commensurate discretion followed from the nature of the case. It was in this light that the proceeding was explained by the Federalist, in words which should be a guide to us now:

The nature of the proceeding can *never be tied down by such strict rules*, either in the delineation of the offence by the prosecutors or in the construction of it by the judges, as in common cases serve to limit the discretion of courts in favor of personal security. (Federalist, No. 65.)

This article was by Alexander Hamilton, writing in concert with James Madison and John Jay. Thus by the highest authority at the adoption of the Constitution we find that impeachment "can never be tied down by strict rules," and that this latitude is applicable to "the delineation of the offence," meaning thereby the procedure or pleading, and also to the "construction of the offence," in both of which cases the "discretion" of the Senate is enlarged beyond that of ordinary courts.

RULES OF EVIDENCE.

From the form of procedure I pass to the *Rules of Evidence*; and here again the Senate must avoid all technicalities and not allow any artificial rule to shut out the truth. It would allow no such thing on the expulsion of a senator. How can it allow any such thing on the expulsion of a President? On this account I voted to admit all evidence that was offered during the trial, believing, in the first place, that it ought to be heard and considered; and, in the second place, that, even if it were shut out from these proceedings, it could not be shut out from the public or be shut out from history, both of which must be the ultimate judges. On the impeachment of Prince Polignac and his colleagues of the cabinet, in 1830, for signing the ordinances which cost Charles X his throne, some forty witnesses were sworn without objection, in a brief space of time, and no testimony was excluded. An examination of the two volumes, entitled *Procès des Derniers Ministres de Charles X* will confirm what I say. This example was to my mind not unworthy of imitation on the present occasion.

There are other rules, which it is not too late to profit by. One of these relates to the burden of proof and is calculated to have a practical bearing. The other relates to matters of which the Senate will take cognizance without any special proof, thus importing into the case unquestionable evidence, which explains and aggravates the transgressions charged.

(1.) Look carefully at the object of this trial. Primarily it is for the expulsion of the President from office. Its motive is not punishment, not vengeance, but the *Public Safety*. Nothing less than this could justify the ponderous proceeding. It will be for the criminal courts to award the punishment due to his offences. The Senate considers only how the safety of the people, which is the supreme law, can be best preserved; and to this end the ordinary rule of evidence is reversed. If on any point you entertain doubts, the benefit of those doubts must be given to your country; and this is the supreme law. When tried on an indictment in the criminal courts Andrew Johnson may justly claim the benefit of your doubts; but at the bar of the Senate on the question of his expulsion from office, his vindication must be in every respect and on each charge beyond a doubt. He must show that his longer continuance in office is not inconsistent with the *Public Safety*:

Or, at least so prove it,
That the probation bear no hinge or loop
To hang a doubt on.

Anything short of this is to trifle with the Republic and its transcendent fortunes.

It is by insisting upon doubts that the apologists of the President, at the bar and in the Senate, seek to save him. For myself, I can see none such, but assuming that they exist, then should they be marshalled for our country. This is not a criminal trial, where the rule prevails: better that many guilty men should escape than one innocent man should suffer. This rule, which is so proper in its place, is not applicable to a proceeding for expulsion from office; and who will undertake to say that any claim of office can be set against the Public Safety?

In thus stating the just rule of evidence, I do little more than apply those time-honored maxims of jurisprudence, which require that every interpretation shall be always in favor of liberty. Early in the common law we were told that he is to be adjudged impious and cruel who does not favor liberty: *impius et crudelis judicandus est qui libertati non favet.* Blackstone, whose personal sympathies were with power, is constrained to confess that "the law is always ready to catch at anything in favor of liberty." (*Blackstone's Commentaries, vol.* 2, *p.* 94.) But liberty and all else are contained in the Public Safety; they depend on the rescue of the country from a presidential usurper. Therefore should we now, in the name of the law, "catch at anything" to save the Republic.

2. There is another rule of evidence which, though of common acceptance in the courts, has peculiar value in this case, where it must exercise a decisive influence. It is this: *Courts will take judicial cognizance of certain matters, without any special proof on the trial.* Some of these are of general knowledge, and others are within the special knowledge of the court. Among these, according to express decision, are the frame of government and the public officers administering it; the accession of the Chief Executive; the sitting of Congress and its usual course of proceeding; the usual course of travel; the ebbs and flows of the tide; *also whatever ought to be generally known within the limits of the jurisdiction, including the history of the country.* Besides these matters of general knowledge a court will take notice of its own records, the conduct of its own officers, and whatever passes in its own presence or under its own eyes. For all this I cite no authority; it is superfluous. I add a single illustration from the great English commentator: "If a contempt be committed in the face of the court, the offender may be instantly apprehended and imprisoned at the discretion of the judges, without any further proof or examination." (*Blackstone's Commentaries, vol.* 4, *p.* 286.)

If this be the rule of courts, *a fortiori* it must be the rule of the Senate on impeachments; for we have seen that, when sitting for this purpose, the Senate enjoys a latitude of its own. Its object is the Public Safety, and, therefore, no aid for the arrival at truth can be rejected. No gate can be closed. But here is a gate opened by the sages of the law and standing open always, to the end that justice may not fail.

Applying this rule to the present proceeding, it will be seen at once how it brings before the Senate, without any further evidence, a long catalogue of crime, affecting the character of the President beyond all possibility of defence, and serving to explain the latter acts on which the impeachment is founded. It was in this chamber, in the face of the Senate and the ministers of foreign powers, and surrounded by the gaze of thronged galleries, that Andrew Johnson exhibited himself in beastly intoxication while he took his oath of office as Vice-President : and all that he has done since is of record here. Much of it appears on our journals. The rest is in authentic documents published by the order of the Senate. Never was a record more complete.

Here in the Senate we know officially how he has made himself the attorney of slavery—the usurper of legislative power—the violator of law—the patron of rebels—the helping hand of rebellion—the kicker from office of good citizens—the open lung-hole of the treasury—the architect of the "whiskey ring"—the stumbling block to all good laws by wanton vetoes and then by criminal hindrances; all these things are known here beyond question. To the apologists of the President, who set up the quibbling objection that they are not alleged in the articles of impeachment, I reply that, even if excluded on this account from judgment, they may be treated as evidence. They are the reservoir from which to draw in determining the true character of the latter acts for which the President is arraigned, and especially the *intent* by which he was animated. If these latter were alone, without connection with the transgressions of the past, they would have remained unnoticed. Impeachment would not have been ordered. It is because they are a prolongation of that wickedness, under which the country has so long suffered, and spring from the same bloody fountain, that they are now presented for judgment. They are not alone ; nor can they be faithfully considered without drawing upon the past. The story of the God Thor in Scandinavian mythology is revived, whose drinking-horn could not be drained by the strongest quaffer, for it communicated with the vast and inexhaustible ocean. Andrew Johnson is our God Thor, and these latter acts for which he stands impeached are the drinking-horn whose depths are unfathomable.

OUTLINE OF TRANSGRESSIONS OF ANDREW JOHNSON.

From this review of the character of this proceeding, showing how it is political in character—before a political body—and with a political judgment, being expulsion from office and nothing more; then how the transgressions of the President, in their protracted line, are embraced under " impeachable offences ;" then how the form of procedure is liberated from the ordinary technicalities of the law ; and lastly how unquestionable rules of evidence open the gates to overwhelming testimony, I pass now to the consideration of this overwhelming testimony and how the present impeachment became a necessity. I have already called it one of the last great battles with slavery. See now how the battle began.

Slavery in all its pretensions is a defiance of law ; for it can have no law in its support. Whoso becomes its representative must act accordingly ; and this is the transcendent crime of Andrew Johnson. For the sake of slavery and to uphold its original supporters in their endeavors to continue this wrong under another name, he has set at defiance the Constitution and laws of the land, and he has accompanied this unquestionable usurpation by brutalities and indecencies in office without precedent, unless we go back to the Roman emperor fiddling, or the French monarch dancing among his minions. This usurpation, with its brutalities and indecencies, became manifest as long ago as the winter of 1866, when, being President, and bound by his oath of office to preserve, protect, and defend the Constitution, and to take care that the laws are faithfully executed, he took to himself legislative powers in the reconstruction of the rebel States, and, in carrying forward this usurpation, nullified an act of Congress, intended as the corner-stone of reconstruction, by virtue of which rebels are excluded from office under the government of the United States, and thereafter, in vindication of this misconduct, uttered a scandalous speech in which he openly charged members of Congress with being assassins, and mentioned some by name. Plainly he should have been impeached and expelled at that early day. The case against him was complete. That great patriot of English history, Lord Somers, has likened impeachment to Goliath's sword hanging in the temple to be taken down only when occasion required; but if ever there was an occasion for its promptest vengeance it was then. Had there been no failure at that time we should be now nearer by two years to restoration of all kinds, whether political or financial. So strong is my conviction of the fatal remissness of the House, that I think the Senate would do a duty in strict harmony with its constitutional place in the government, and the analogies of judicial tribunals so often adduced, if it reprimanded the House of Representatives for this delay. Of course the Senate could not originate an impeachment. It could not take down the sword of Goliath. It must wait on the House, as the court waits on the grand jury. But this waiting has cost the country more than can be told.

Meanwhile the President proceeded in his transgressions. There is nothing of usurpation which he has not attempted. Beginning with an assumption of all power in the rebel States, he has shrunk from nothing in the maintenance of this unparalleled assumption. This is a plain statement of fact. Timid at first, he grew bolder and bolder. He saw too well that his attempt to substitute himself for Congress in the work of reconstruction was sheer usurpation, and, therefore, by his Secretary of State, did not hesitate to announce that "it must be distinctly understood that the restoration will be *subject to the decision of Congress.*" On two separate occasions, in July and September, 1865, he confessed the power of Congress over the subject; but when Congress came together in December, this confessor of congressional power found that he alone had this great prerogative. According to his new-fangled theory, Congress had nothing to do but admit the States with the governments which had been instituted through his will alone. It is difficult to measure the vastness of this usurpation, involving as it did a general nullification. Strafford was not bolder, when, speaking for Charles I, he boasted that "the little finger of prerogative was heavier than the loins of the law;" but these words helped the proud minister to the scaffold. No monarch, no despot, no Sultan, could claim more than an American President; for he claimed all. By his edict alone governments were organized, taxes were levied, and even the franchises of the citizen were determined.

Had this assumption of power been incidental, for the exigency of the moment, as under the pressure of war, and especially to serve the cause of human rights, to which before his elevation the President had professed such vociferous devotion, it might have been pardoned. It would have passed into the chapter of unauthorized acts which a patriot people had condoned. But it was the opposite in every particular. Beginning and continuing in usurpation, it was hateful beyond pardon, because it sacrificed the rights of Unionists, white and black, and was in the interest of the rebellion and of those very rebels who had been in arms against their country.

More than one person was appointed provisional governor who could not take the oath of office required by act of Congress. Other persons in the same predicament were appointed in the revenue service. The effect of these appointments was disastrous. They were in the nature of notice to rebels everywhere, that participation in the rebellion was no bar to office. If one of their number could be appointed governor, if another could be appointed to a confidential position in the Treasury Department, then there was nobody on the long list of blood who might not look for preferment. And thus all offices from governor to constable were handed over to a disloyal scramble. Rebels crawled forth from their retreats. Men who had hardly ventured to expect their lives were now candidates for office, and the rebellion became strong again. The change was felt in all the gradations of government, whether in States, counties, towns, or villages. Rebels found themselves in places of trust, while the true-hearted Unionists, who had watched for the coming of our flag and ought to have enjoyed its protecting power, were driven into hiding-places. All this was under the auspices of Andrew Johnson. It was he who animated the wicked crew. He was at the head of the work. Loyalty everywhere was persecuted. White and black, whose only offence was that they had been true to their country, were insulted, abused, murdered. There was no safety for the loyal man except within the flash of our bayonets. The story is as authentic as hideous. More than two thousand murders have been reported in Texas alonesince the surrender of Kirby Smith In other States there was a similar carnival. Property, person, life, were all in jeopardy. Acts were done "to make a holiday in hell." At New Orleans there was a fearful massacre, which, considering the age and the place, was worse than that of St. Bartholomew, which darkens a century of France, or that of Glencoe, which has printed an ineffaceable stain upon one of the greatest reigns of English history. All this is directly traced to Andrew Johnson. The words of bitterness uttered at another time are justified, while Fire, Famine, and Slaughter shriek forth—

He let me loose, and cried Halloo !
To him alone the praise is due.

ACCUMULATION OF IMPEACHABLE OFFENCES.

This is nothing but the outline, derived from historic sources *which the Senate on this occasion is bound to recognize.* Other acts fall within the picture. The officers he had appointed in defiance of law were paid also in the same defiance. Millions of property were turned over without consideration to railroad companies, whose special recommendation was their participation in the rebellion. The Freedman's Bureau, that sacred charity of the Republic, was despoiled of its possessions for the sake of rebels, to whom their forfeited estates were given back after they had been vested by law in the United States. The proceeds of captured and abandoned property, lodged under the law in the national treasury, were ravished from their place of deposit and sacrificed. Rebels were allowed to fill the ante-chambers of the Executive Mansion and to enter into his counsels. The pardoning power was prostituted, and pardons were issued in lots to suit rebels, thus grossly abusing that trust whose discreet exercise is so essential to the administration of justice. The powers of the Senate over appointments were trifled with and disregarded by reappointing persons who had been already rejected, and by refusing to communicate the names of others appointed by him during the recess. The veto power conferred by the Constitution as a remedy for ill-considered legislation, was turned by him into a weapon of offence against Congress and into an instrument to beat down the just opposition which his usurpation had aroused. The power of removal, which patriot Presidents had exercised so sparingly, was seized as an engine of tyranny and openly employed to maintain his wicked purposes by the sacrifice of good citizens who would not consent to be his tools. Incompetent and dishonest creatures, whose only recommendation was that they echoed his voice, were appointed to office, especially in the collection of the internal revenue, through whom a new organization, known as the "Whisky Ring," has been able to prevail over the government and to rob the treasury of millions at the cost of tax-paying citizens, whose burdens are thus increased. Laws enacted by Congress for the benefit of the colored race, including that great statute for the establishment of the Freedmen's Bureau, and that other great statute for the establishment of Civil Rights, were first attacked by his veto, and, when finally passed by the requisite majority over his veto, were treated by him as little better than dead letters, while he boldly attempted to prevent the adoption of a constitutional amendment, by which the right of citizens and the national debt were placed under the guarantee of irrepealable law. During these successive assumptions, usurpations, and tyrannies, utterly without precedent in our history, this deeply guilty man ventured upon public speeches, each an offence to good morals, where, lost to all shame, he appealed in coarse words to the coarse passions of the coarsest people, scattering firebrands of sedition, inflaming anew the rebel spirit, insulting good citizens, and, with regard to office-holders, announcing in his own characteristic phrase that he would "kick them out"—the whole succession of speeches being from their brutalities and indecencies in the nature of a "criminal exposure of his person," indictable at common law, for which no judgment can be too severe. But even this revolting transgression is aggravated, when it is considered that through these utterances the cause of justice was imperiled and the accursed demon of civil feud was lashed again into vengeful fury. All these things from beginning to end are plain facts, already recorded in history and known to all. And it is further recorded in history and known to all, that, through these enormities, any one of which is enough for condemnation, while all together present an aggregation of crime, untold calamities have been brought upon our country ; disturbing business and finance ; diminishing the national revenues ; postponing specie payments ; dishonoring the Declaration of Independence in its grandest truths ; arresting the restoration of the rebel States ; reviving the dying rebellion, and instead of that peace and reconciliation so much longed for, sowing strife and wrong, whose natural fruit is violence and blood.

OPEN DEFIANCE OF CONGRESS.

For all these, or any one of them, Andrew Johnson should have been impeached and expelled from office. The case required a statement only ; not an argument. Unhappily this was not done. As a petty substitute for the judgment which should have been pronounced, and as a bridle on presidential tyranny in "kicking out of office," Congress enacted a law known as the tenure-of-office act, passed March 2, 1867, over his veto by the vote of two-thirds of both houses. And in order to prepare the way for impeachment, by removing certain scruples of technicality, its violation was expressly declared to be a high misdemeanor.

The President began at once to chafe under its restraint. Recognizing the act and following its terms, he first suspended Mr. Stanton from office, and then, on his restoration by the Senate, made an attempt to win General Grant into a surrender of the department, so as to oust Mr. Stanton and to render the restoration by the Senate ineffectual. Meanwhile Sheridan in Louisiana, Pope in Alabama, and Sickles in South Carolina, who, as military commanders, were carrying into the pacification of these States all the energies which had been so brilliantly displayed in the war, were pursued by the same vindictive spirit. They were removed by the President, and rebellion throughout that whole region clapped its hands. This was done in the exercise of his power as Commander-in-chief. At last, in his unappeased rage, he openly violated the tenure-of-office act, so as to bring himself under its judgment, by the defiant attempt to remove Mr. Stanton from the War Department. without the consent of the Senate, and the appointment of Lorenzo Thomas, Adjutant General of the United States, as Secretary of War ad interim.

IMPEACHMENT AT LAST.

The Grand Inquest of the nation, which had slept on so many enormities, was awakened by this open defiance. The gauntlet was flung into its very chamber, and there it lay on the floor. The President, who had already claimed everything for the Executive with impunity, now rushed into conflict with Congress on the very ground selected in advance by the latter. The field was narrow, but sufficient. There was but one thing for the House of Representatives to do. Andrew Johnson must be impeached, or the tenure-of-office act would become a dead letter, while his tyranny would receive a letter of license, and impeachment as a remedy for wrong-doing would be blotted from the Constitution.

Accordingly it was resolved that the offender, whose crimes had so long escaped judgment, should be impeached. Once entered upon this work, the House of Representatives, after setting forth the removal of Mr. Stanton and the appointment of General Thomas in violation of the law and Constitution, proceeded further to charge him in different forms with conspiracy wrongfully to get possession of the War Department; also with an attempt to corrupt General Emory and induce him to violate an act of Congress; also with scandalous speeches, such as no President could be justified in making; concluding with a general article setting forth attempts on his part to prevent the execution of certain acts of Congress.

Such is a simple narrative, which brings us to the articles of impeachment. Nothing that I have said thus far is superfluous; for it shows the origin of this proceeding, and illustrates its moving cause. The articles themselves are narrow, if not technical. But they are filled and broadened by the transgressions of the past, all of which enter into the present offences. The whole is an unbroken series with a common life. As well separate the Siamese twins as separate the offences now charged from that succession of antecedent crimes with which they are linked, any one of which is enough for judgment. The present springs from the past and can be truly seen only in its light, which, in this case, is nothing less than "darkness visible."

ARTICLES OF IMPEACHMENT.

In entering upon the discussion of the articles of impeachment, I confess my regret that so great a cause, on which so much depends, should be presented on such narrow ground, although I cannot doubt that the whole past must be taken into consideration in determining the character of the acts alleged. If there has been a violation of the Constitution and laws, the apologists of the President then insist that all was done with good intentions. In reply to this it is enough if we point to the past, which thus becomes a part of the case. But of this hereafter. It is unnecessary for me to take time in setting forth the articles. The abstract already presented is enough. They will naturally come under review before the close of the inquiry.

Of the transactions embraced by the articles, the removal of Mr. Stanton has unquestionably attracted the most attention, although I cannot doubt that the scandalous harangues are as justly worthy of condemnation. But the former has been made the pivot of this impeachment; so much so that the whole case seems to revolve on this transaction. Therefore I shall not err, if, following the articles, I put this foremost in the present inquiry.

This transaction may be brought to the touchstone of the Constitution, and also of the tenure-of-office act. But since the allegation of a violation of this act has been so conspicuous, and this act may be regarded as a congressional interpretation of the power of removals under the Constitution, I begin with the consideration of the questions arising under it.

TENURE-OF-OFFICE ACT.

The general object of the tenure-of-office act was to protect civil officers from removal without the advice and consent of the Senate; and it was made in express terms applicable to "every person holding any civil office to which he has been appointed by and with the advice and consent of the Senate." To this provision, so broad in its character, was appended a proviso as follows:

Provided, That the Secretaries of State, of the Treasury, of War, of the Navy, and of the Interior, the Postmaster General, and the Attorney General shall hold their offices respectively for and during the term of the President by whom they may have been appointed and for one month thereafter, subject to removal by and with the advice and consent of the Senate.

As this general protection from removal without the advice and consent of the Senate might be productive of embarrassment during the recess of the Senate, it was further provided, in a second section, that during such recess any person may be suspended from office by the President on reasons assigned, which it is made his duty to report to the Senate within twenty days after its next meeting, and if the Senate concurs, then the President may remove the officer and appoint a successor; but if the Senate does not concur, then the suspended officer shall forthwith resume his functions.

On this statute two questions arise: first as to its constitutionality, and secondly as to its application to Mr. Stanton, so as to protect him from removal without the advice and consent of the Senate. It is impossible not to confess in advance that both have been already practically settled. The statute was passed over the veto of the President by a vote of two-thirds, who thus solemnly united in declaring its constitutionality. Then came the suspension of Mr. Stanton, and his restoration to office by a triumphant vote of the Senate, being no less than 35 to 6, thus establishing not only the constitutionality of the statute, but also its protecting application to Mr. Stanton. And then came the resolution of the Senate, adopted after protracted debate on the 21st February, by a vote of 27 to 6, declaring, that, under the Constitution and laws of the United States, the President has no power to remove the Secretary of War and to designate any other officer to perform the duties of that office *ad interim*; thus for the third time affirming the constitutionality of the statute, and for the second time its protecting application to Mr. Stanton. There is no instance in our history where there has been such a succession of votes, with such large majorities, declaring the conclusions of the Senate and fixing them beyond recall. "Thrice is he armed who hath his quarrel just;" but the tenure-of-office act is armed *thrice* by the votes of the Senate. The apologists of the President seem to say of these solemn votes, "Thrice the brinded cat hath mewed;" but such a three-fold record of the Senate cannot be treated with levity.

The question of the constitutionality of this statute complicates itself with the power of removal under the Constitution; but I shall not consider the latter question at this stage It will naturally present itself when we consider the power of removal under the Constitution which has been claimed by the President. For the present I assume the constitutionality of the statute.

ITS APPLICATION TO MR. STANTON.

I come at once to the question of the application of the statute to Mr. Stanton, so as to protect him against removal without the consent of the Senate. And here I doubt if any question would have arisen but for the hasty words of the senator from Ohio, [Mr. Sherman,] so often quoted in this proceeding.

Unquestionably the senator from Ohio, when the report of the conference committee of the two houses was under discussion, stated that the statute did not protect Mr. Stanton in his office; but this was the individual opinion of this senator, and nothing more. On hearing it I cried from my seat, "The senator

2 Sumner

must speak for himself;" for I held the opposite opinion. It was clear to my mind that the statute was intended to protect Mr. Stanton, and that it did protect him. The senator from Oregon, [Mr. Williams,] who was the chairman of the conference committee and conducted its deliberations, informs us that there was no suggestion in the committee that the statute did not protect all of the President's cabinet, including, of course, Mr. Stanton. The debates in the House of Representatives are the same way. Without undertaking to hold the scales in which to weigh any such conflicting opinions, I rest on the received rule of law that they cannot be taken into account in determining the meaning of the statute. And here I quote the judgment of the Supreme Court of the United States, pronounced by Chief Justice Taney :

In expounding this law, the judgment of *the court cannot in any degree be influenced by the construction placed upon it by individual members of Congress in the debate which took place on its passage*, nor by the motives or reasons assigned by them for supporting or opposing amendments that were offered. The law that passed is the will of the majority of both houses, and the only mode in which that will is spoken is in the act itself; and we must gather their intention from the language there used, comparing it, when any ambiguity exists, with the laws upon the same subject, and *looking, if necessary, to the public history of the times in which it was passed.* (*Aldridge* vs. *Williams*, 3 Howard's Rep., 24.)

It is obvious to all acquainted with a legislative body that the rule thus authoritatively declared is the only one that could be safely applied. The Senate in construing the present statute must follow this rule. Therefore, I repair to the statute, stopping for a moment to glance at the public history of the times, in order to understand its object.

Already, we have seen how the President, in carrying forward his usurpation in the interest of the rebellion, has trifled with the Senate in regard to appointments, and abused the traditional power of removal, openly threatening good citizens in office that he would "kick them out," and filling all vacancies, from high to low, with creatures whose first promise was to sustain his barbarous policy. I do not stop to portray the extent of this outrage, constituting an impeachable offence, according to the declared opinion of Mr. Madison, one of the strongest advocates of the presidential power of removal. Congress, instead of adopting the remedy, suggested by this father of the Constitution, and expelling the President by process of impeachment, attempted to wrest from him the power he was abusing. For this purpose the tenure-of-office act was passed. It was deemed advisable to include the cabinet officers within its protection; but, considering the intimate relations between them and the President, a proviso was appended securing to the latter the right of choosing them in the first instance. Its object was, where the President finds himself, on accession to office, confronted by a hostile Senate to secure to him this right of choice, without obliging him to keep the cabinet of his predecessor; and accordingly it says to him, "Choose your own cabinet, but expect to abide by your choice, unless you can obtain the consent of the Senate to a change."

Any other conclusion is flat absurdity. It begins by misconstruing the operative words of the proviso, that the cabinet officers "shall hold their offices respectively for and during the term of the President by whom they are appointed." On its face there is no ambiguity here. It is only by going outside that any can be found, and this disappears on a brief inquiry. At the date of the statute Andrew Johnson had been in office two years. Some of his cabinet were originally appointed by President Lincoln ; others had been formally appointed by himself. *But all were there equally by his approval and consent.* One may do an act himself, or make it his own by ratifying it when done by another. In law it is equally his act. Andrew Johnson did not originally appoint Mr. Stanton, Mr. Seward, or Mr. Welles, but he adopted their appointments, so that at the passage of the statute they stood on the same footing as if originally appointed by him. *Practically and in the sense of the statute, they were appointed by him.* They were a cabinet of his own choice, just as much as the cabinet of his successor, duly appointed, will be of his own choice. If the statute compels the latter, as it clearly does, to abide by his choice, it is unreasonable to suppose that it is not equally obligatory on Andrew Johnson. Otherwise we find a special immunity for that President whose misconduct rendered it necessary, and Congress is exhibited as legislating for some future unknown President, and not for Andrew Johnson, already too well known.

Even the presidential apologists do not question that the members of the cabinet commissioned by Andrew Johnson are protected by the statute. How grossly unreasonable to suppose that Congress intended to make such a distinction among his cabinet as to protect those whose support of his usurpation had gained them seats which they enjoyed, while it exposed to his caprice a great citizen, whose faithful services during the war had won the gratitude of his country, whose continuance in office was regarded as an assurance of public safety, and whose attempted removal has been felt as a national calamity. Clearly, then, it was the intention of the statute to protect the whole cabinet, whether originally appointed by Andrew Johnson or originally appointed by his predecessor and continued by him.

I have no hesitation in saying that no other conclusion is possible without doing violence to the statute. I cannot forget that, while we are permitted "to open the law on doubts," we are solemnly warned "not to open doubts on the law." It is Lord Bacon who gives us this rule, whose obvious meaning is, that where doubts do not exist they should not be invented. It is only by this forbidden course that any question can be raised. If we look at the statute in its simplicity, its twofold object is apparent : first, to prohibit removals ; and secondly, to limit certain terms of service. *The prohibition to remove plainly applies to all. The limitation of service applies only to members of the cabinet.* I agree with the excellent senator from Iowa [Mr. Harlan] that this analysis removes all ambiguity. The pretension that any one of the cabinet was left to the unchecked power of the President is irreconcilable with the concluding words of the proviso, which declares that they shall "be subject to removal by and with the advice and consent of the Senate;" thus expressly excluding the prerogative of the President.

Let us push this inquiry still further by looking more particularly at the statute, reduced to a skeleton, so that we may see its bones. It is as follows :

(1.) *Every person holding any civil office,* by and with the advice and consent of the Senate, shall be entitled to hold such office until a successor is appointed.

(2.) If members of the cabinet, *then during the term of the President by whom they may have been appointed* and one month thereafter, unless sooner removed by consent of the Senate.

Mr. Stanton obviously falls within the general class, "every person holding any civil office ;" and he is entitled to the full benefit of the provision for their benefit.

As obviously he falls within the sub-class, "members of the cabinet."

In this latter class his rights are equally clear. It is in the discussions under this head that the ingenuity of lawyers has found the amplest play, mainly turning upon what is meant by "term" in the statute. I glance for a moment at some of these theories.

(1.) One pretension is that the "term," having expired with the life of President Lincoln, Mr. Stanton is retroactively legislated out of office on the 15th May, 1865. As this is a penal statute, this construction makes it *ex post facto,* and therefore unconstitutional. It also makes Congress enact this absurdity that Mr. Stanton had for two years been holding office illegally, whereas he had been holding under the clearest legal title, which could no more be altered by legislation than black could be made white. A construction which makes the statute at once unconstitutional and absurd must be rejected.

(2.) The quibble that would exclude Mr. Stanton from the protection of the statute, because he was appointed during the first "term" of President Lincoln, and the statute does not speak of "terms," is hardly worthy of notice. It leads to the same absurd results as follow from the first supposition, enhanced by increasing the retroactive effect.

(3.) Assuming that the statute does not terminate Mr. Stanton's right a month after President Linc ln's death, it is insisted that it must take effect at the earliest possible moment, and therefore on its passage. From this it follows that Mr. Stanton has been illegally in office since the 2d March, 1867, and that both he and the President have been guilty of a violation of law, the former in exercising the duties of an office to which he had no right, and the latter for appointing him, or continuing him, in office, without the consent of the Senate, in violation of the Constitution and the statute in question. Here is another absurdity to be rejected.

(4.) Assuming, as it is easy to do, that it is President Lincoln's "term," we have the better theory, that it did not expire with his life, but continues until the 4th of March, 1869, in which event Mr. Stanton is clearly entitled to hold until a month thereafter. This construction is entirely reasonable and in harmony with the Constitution and legislation under it. I confess that it is one to which I have often inclined.

This brings me back to the construction with which I began, and I find Andrew Johnson is the President who appointed Mr. Stanton. To make this simple, it is only necessary to read "chosen" for "appointed" in the statute, or, if you please, consider the continuance of Mr. Stanton in office, with the concurrence of the President, as a practical appointment or equivalent thereto. Clearly Mr. Stanton was in office, when the statute passed, from the "choice" of the President. Otherwise he would have been removed. His continuance was like another commission. This carries out the intention of the framers of the statute, violates no sound canon of construction, and is entirely reasonable in every respect. Or, if preferred, we may consider the "term" to be that of President Lincoln, and then Mr. Stanton would be protected in office until one month after the 4th of March next. But whether the "term" be of Andrew Johnson or of President Lincoln, he is equally protected.

Great efforts have been made to show that Mr. Stanton does not come within the special protection of the proviso, without considering the irresistible consequence that he is then within the general protection of the statute, being "a person holding a civil office." Turn him out of the proviso and he falls into the statute, unless you are as imaginative as one of the apologists, who placed him in a sort of intermediate limbo, like a lost spirit floating in space, as in one of Flaxman's Illustrations of Dante. But the imagination of this conception cannot make us insensible to its surpassing absurdity. It is utterly unreasonable, and every construction must be rejected which cannot stand the touchstone of common sense.

THE SUSPENSION OF MR. STANTON RECOGNIZED HIM AS PROTECTED BY THE STATUTE.

Here I might close this part of the case; but there is still another illustration. In suspending Mr. Stanton from office, as long ago as August, the President himself recognized that he was protected by the statute. The facts are familiar. The President, in formal words, undertook to say that the suspension was by virtue of the Constitution; but this was a dishonest pretext in harmony with so much in his career. Whatever he may say, his acts speak louder than his words. In sending notice of the suspension to the Secretary of the Treasury, and then again in sending a message to the Senate assigning his reasons for the suspension, both being according to the requirements of the statute, he testified that, in his judgment at that time, Mr. Stanton came within its protection. If not, why thus elaborately comply with its requirements? Why the notice to the Secretary of the Treasury? Why the reasons to the Senate? All this was novel and without example. Why write to General Grant of " being sustained " by the Senate? The approval or disapproval of the Senate could make no difference in the exercise of the power which he now sets up. The approval could not confirm the suspension; the disapproval could not restore the suspended Secretary of War. In fine, why suspend at all? Why exercise the power of suspension when the President sets up the power of removal? If Mr. Stanton was unfit for office and a thorn in his side, why not remove him at once? Why resort to this long and untried experiment merely to remove at last? There is but one answer. Beyond all question the President thought Mr. Stanton protected by the statute, and sought to remove him according to its provisions, beginning, therefore, with his suspension. Failing in this, he undertook to remove him in contravention of the statute, relying in justification on his pretension to judge of its constitutionality, or the pusillanimity of Congress, or something else "to turn up," which should render justification unnecessary.

Clearly the suspension was made under the tenure-of-office act and can be justified in no other way. From this conclusion the following dilemma results: If Mr. Stanton was within the statute, by what right was he removed? If he was not, by what right was he suspended? The President may choose his horn. Either will be sufficient to convict.

I should not proceed further under this head but for the new device, which makes its appearance under the auspices of the senator from Maine, [Mr. Fessenden,] who tells us that "whether Mr. Stanton came under the first section of the statute or not, the President had a clear right to suspend him under the second." Thus, a statute, intended as a bridle on the President, gives to the President the power to suspend Mr. Stanton, but fails to give to Mr. Stanton any protection against the President. This statement would seem to be enough. The invention of the senator is not less fallacious than the pretext of the President. It is a device well calculated to help the President and to hurt Mr. Stanton, with those who regard devices more than the reason of the statute and its spirit.

Study the statute in its reason and its spirit, and you cannot fail to see that the second section was intended merely as a pendant to the first, and was meant to apply to the cases included in the first, and none other. It was a sort of safety-valve or contrivance to guard against the possible evils from bad men, who could not be removed during the recess of the Senate. There was no reason to suspend a person who could be removed. It is absurd to suppose that a President would resort to a dilatory and roundabout suspension, when the short cut of removal was open to him. Construing the statute by this plain reason, its second section must have precisely the same sphere of operation as the first. By the letter, Mr. Stanton falls within both; by the intention, it is the same. It is only by applying to the first section his own idea of the intention, and by availing himself of the letter of the second, that the senator is able to limit the one and to enlarge the other, so as to exclude Mr. Stanton from the protection of the statute, and to include him in the part allowing suspensions. Applying either letter or spirit consistently, the case is plain.

I turn for the present from the tenure-of-office act, insisting that Mr. Stanton is within its protection, and being so, that his removal was, under the circumstances, a high misdemeanor, aggravated by its defiant purpose and the long series of transgressions which preceded it, all showing a criminal intent. The apologies of the President will be considered hereafter.

The case of Mr. Stanton has two branches : first, his removal, and, secondly, the substitution of General Thomas as Secretary of War *ad interim*. As the first was contrary to positive statute, so also was the latter without support in the acts of Congress. For the present I content myself with this latter proposition, without opening the question of the powers of the President under the Constitution.

The offender rests his case on the act of Congress of February 13, 1795, (1 *Statutes at Large*, 415,) which authorizes the President, "in case of *vacancy* in the office of Secretary of War, whereby he cannot perform the duties of said office," to appoint "any person" until a successor be appointed or such vacancy be filled ; and the supply of the vacancy is limited to six months. Under this early statute the President defends himself by insisting that there was a "vacancy," when, in fact, there was none. All this is in that unfailing spirit of prerogative which is his guide. Here is an assumption of power. In point of fact, Mr. Stanton was at his office quietly discharging its duties when the President assumed that there was a "vacancy," and forthwith sent the valiant Adjutant General to enter upon possession. The assumption and the commission were on a par. There is nothing in any law of the land to sanction either. Each testifies against the offender.

The hardihood of this proceeding becomes more apparent, when it is understood that this very statute of 1795, on which the offender relies, was repealed by the statute of February 20, 1863, passed in our own day, and freshly remembered by many of us. The latter statute, by necessary implication, obliterated the former. Such is the obvious intention, and I do not hesitate to say that any other construction leads into those absurdities which constitute the staple of the presidential apologists. The object of Congress was to provide a substitute for previous statutes, restricting at once the number of vacancies which might be filled and the persons who might fill them. And this was done.

As by the Constitution all appointments must receive the consent of the Senate, therefore any legislation in derogation thereof must be construed strictly ; but the President insists that it shall be extended even in face of the constitutional requirement. To such pretensions is he driven. The exception recognized by the Constitution is only where a vacancy occurs during the recess of the Senate, when the President is authorized to appoint until he can obtain the consent of the Senate and no longer. It is obvious, however, that cases may arise where a sudden accident vacates the office or where the incumbent is temporarily disabled. Here was the occasion for an *ad interim* appointment, and the repealing statute embodying the whole law of the subject, was intended to provide for such cases ; securing to the President time to select a successor, and also power to provide for a temporary disability. Such is the underlying principle of this statute, which it is for us to apply on the present occasion. The expiration of a commission, which ordinary care can foresee, is not one of these sudden emergencies for which provision must be made ; and, assuming that vacancies by removal were contemplated, which must be denied, it is plain that the delay required for the examination of the case would give time to select a successor, while a removal without cause would never be made until a successor was ready.

Look now at the actual facts and you will see how little they come within the reason of an *ad interim* appointment. Evidently the President had resolved to remove Mr. Stanton last summer. Months passed, and he did not consummate his purpose till February. All the intervening time was his to select a successor, being a period longer than the longest fixed for the duration of an *ad interim* appointment by the very statutes under which he professed to act. In conversation with General Sherman, a month before the removal, he showed that he was then looking for a successor *ad interim*. Why not a *permanent* successor?

It took him only a day to find Mr. Ewing. If, as there is reason to suppose, Mr. Ewing was already selected, when General Thomas was pushed forward, *why appoint General Thomas at all?* Why not, in the usual way, transmit Mr. Ewing's name as the successor? For the excellent reason, that the offender knew the Senate would not confirm him, and that, therefore, Mr. Stanton would remain in office; whereas through an *ad interim* appointment he might obtain possession of the War Department, which was his end and aim. The *ad interim* appointment of General Thomas was, therefore, an attempt to obtain possession of an office without the consent of the Senate, precisely *because the offender knew that he could not obtain that consent.* And all this was under the pretext of an act of Congress, which, alike in letter and spirit, was inapplicable to the case.

Thus does it appear, that, while Mr. Stanton was removed in violation of the tenure-of-office act, General Thomas was appointed Secretary of War *ad interim* in equal derogation of the acts of Congress regulating the subject.

REMOVAL AND SUBSTITUTION AD INTERIM A VIOLATION OF THE CONSTITUTION.

It remains to consider if the removal and substitution were not each in violation of the Constitution. The case is new, for never until now could it arise. Assuming that the tenure-of-office act does not protect Mr. Stanton, who is thus left afloat in the limbo between the body of the act and the proviso, then the President is remitted to his prerogative under the Constitution, and he must be judged accordingly, independent of statute. Finding the power of removal there, he may be justified; but not finding it there, he must bear the consequences. And here *the tenure-of-office act furnishes a living and practical construction of the Constitution from which there is no appeal.*

From the Constitution it appears that the power of appointment is vested in the President and Senate conjointly, and that nothing is said of the power of removal, except in case of impeachment, when it is made by the Senate. Therefore, the power of removal is not express, but implied only, and must exist, if at all, as a necessary consequence of the power to appoint. In whom must it exist? It is a familiar rule that the power which makes can unmake. Unless this rule be rejected, the power of removal must exist in the President and Senate conjointly; nor is there anything unreasonable in this conclusion. Removal can always be effected during the session of the Senate by the nomination and confirmation of a successor, while provision can be made for the recess by an act of Congress. This conclusion would be irresistible, were the Senate always in session, but since it is not, and since cases may arise during the recess requiring the immediate exercise of this power of removal, it has been argued that at least during the recess it must be in the President alone. From this position there has been a jump to the next, and it has been insisted that since, for the sake of public convenience, the power of removal exists in the President, he is at liberty to exercise it, either during the recess or the session itself. Here is an obvious extension of the conclusion which the premises do not warrant. The reason failing the conclusion must fail. *Cessante ratione cessat etiam ipsa lex.* Especially must this be the case under the Constitution. A power founded on implied necessity must fail when that necessity does not exist. The implication cannot be carried beyond the reason. Therefore, the power of removal during the recess, doubtful at best unless sanctioned by act of Congress, cannot be extended to justify the exercise of that power while the Senate is in session, ready to act conjointly with the President.

Against this natural conclusion we have the assumption that a contrary construction of the Constitution was established after debate in 1789. I avoid all details with regard to this debate which has been considered and cited so often. I content myself by asking if at best it was anything but a congressional construction of the Constitution, and, as such, subject to be set aside by another voice from

the same quarter. It was, moreover, a congressional construction adopted during
the administration of Washington, whose personal character must have influenced opinion largely; and it prevailed in the House of Representatives only
after earnest debate, by a bare majority, and in the Senate only by the casting
vote of the Vice-President, John Adams, who, from position as well as principle,
was not inclined to shear the President of any prerogative. Once adopted, and
no strong necessity for a change occurring, it was allowed to go unaltered, but
not unquestioned. Jurists like Kent and Story, statesmen like Webster, Clay,
Calhoun, and Benton, recorded themselves adversely, and it was once reversed
by the vote of the Senate. This was in 1835, when a bill passed the Senate,
reported by Mr. Calhoun and sustained by the ablest statesmen of the time,
practically denying the power of the President. The tenure-of-office act was
heralded in 1863 by a statute making the Comptroller of the Currency removable
"by and with the advice and consent of the Senate," thus, in this individual
case, asserting for the Senate a check on the President; and then in 1866, by
a more important measure, being the provision in the army appropriation act,
that "no military or naval officer shall be dismissed except upon the sentence
of a court-martial;" thus putting another check on the President. Finally, this
congressional construction, born of a casting vote, and questioned ever since,
has been overruled by another congressional construction, which has been twice
adopted in both houses, first by large majorities on the original passage of the
tenure of-office act, and then by a vote of two-thirds on the final passage of the
same act over the veto of the President; and then again adopted by a vote of
more than two-thirds of the Senate, when the latter condemned the removal of
Mr. Stanton; and all this in the light of experience, after ample debate, and
with all the consequences before them. Such a congressional construction must
have a controlling influence, and the fact that it reversed the practice of eighty
years and overcame the disposition to stand on the ancient ways, would seem
to increase rather than diminish its weight.

Now, mark the consequences. Originally, in 1789, there was a congressional
construction, which, in effect, made the Constitution read:

The President *shall have* the power of removal.

For the next eighty years all removals were made under this construction.
The tenure-of-office act was a new congressional construction, overruling the
first and entitled to equal if not superior weight. By virtue of this congressional construction, the Constitution now reads:

The President *shall not have* the power of removal.

It follows, then, that in removing Mr. Stanton the President violated the Constitution as now construed.

The dilemma is this: If the President can remove Mr. Stanton during the
session of the Senate, without any power by statute, it is only by virtue of a
prerogative vested in him by the Constitution, which must necessarily override
the tenure-of-office act, as an unconstitutional effort to abridge it. If, on the
other hand, this act is constitutional, the prerogative of removal is not in the
President, and he violated the Constitution when he assumed to exercise it.

The tenure-of-office act cannot be treated otherwise than constitutional. Certainly not in the Senate, where some among the apologists of the President
voted for it. Therefore the prerogative of removal is not in the President.
The long practice which grew up under a mere reading of the Constitution,
has been declared erroneous. To this extent the Constitution has been amended,
and it is as absurd to plead the practice under the first reading in order to justify an offence under the second, as to plead the existence of slavery before the
constitutional amendment in order to justify this monstrosity now.

Thus must we conclude that the offender has not only violated the tenure-of-
office act, but also the Constitution; that, even assuming that Mr. Stanton is
not protected by the statute, the case is not ended; that this statute, if con-

strued so as to exclude him, cannot be rejected as a congressional construction of the Constitution; and that, under this congressional construction, which in value is second only to a constitutional amendment, the prerogative of removal without the consent of the Senate does not belong to the President. Of course the power of suspension under the Constitution, which is only an incident of the larger pretension, must fall also. Therefore, in the defiant removal of Mr. Stanton, and also in the pretended suspension under the Constitution with which the transaction began, the President violated the Constitution, and was guilty of an impeachable offence.

And so, also, we must conclude that, in the substitution of Lorenzo Thomas as Secretary of War *ad interim*, the offender violated not only the acts of Congress for the supply of vacancies, but also the Constitution. Knowing that he could not obtain possession of the office with the consent of the Senate, he sought to accomplish this purpose without that consent. Thus, under color of a statute, he practically set the Constitution at defiance. Mark here his inconsistency. He violates the tenure-of-office act, alleging that it is against the Constitution, whose champion he professes to be, and then takes advantage of the acts of Congress for the supply of vacancies to set aside the Constitution in one of its most important requirements; for all which he is justly charged with an impeachable offence.

All this seems clear. Any other conclusion gives to the President the power under the Constitution to vacate all national offices and leaves the republic the wretched victim of tyranny, with a ruler who is not even a constitutional monarch, but a king above all laws. It was solemnly alleged in the articles against Charles I of England, that "being admitted king of England, and therein trusted with a limited power *to govern by and according to the laws of the land and* NOT OTHERWISE," he nevertheless undertook " *to rule according to his will* and to overthrow the rights and liberties of the people." These very words might be adopted now to declare the crime of Andrew Johnson.

THE APOLOGIES.

Here I might close; but the offender has found apologists, who plead his cause at the bar and in the Senate. The apologies are a strange compound, enlarging rather than diminishing the offences proved. There is, first, the Apology of Good Intentions; next, the Apology of making a case for the Supreme Court, being the Moot Court Apology; and, then, the Apology that the President may sit in judgment on the laws, and determine whether they shall be executed, which I call the Apology of Prerogative. Following these is a swarm of technicalities, devices, and quibbles, utterly unworthy of the Senate, and to be reprobated by all who love justice.

THE APOLOGY OF GOOD INTENTIONS.

I begin with the Apology of *Good Intentions*. In the light of all that has occurred, with the volume of history open before us, with the records of the Senate in our hands, and with the evidence at the bar not utterly forgotten, it is inconceivable that such an apology can be put forward. While making it the apologists should be veiled, so that the derisive smile on their faces may not be observed by the Senate, to whose simplicity it is addressed. It is hard to treat this apology; but it belongs to the case, and therefore I deal with it.

Of course a mere technical violation of law, with no evil consequences and without any claim of title, is followed by nominal damages only. If a person steps on a field of grass belonging to another, without permission, he is a trespasser, and the law furnishes a familiar proceeding against him; but if he has done this accidentally, and without any real damage, it would be hard to pursue him, unless the assertion of the title were thought important. But if this trespasser is an old offender, who from the beginning has broken fences, ruined trees, and trampled down the garden, and who now defiantly comes upon the field of grass, insisting upon absolute ownership, then it is vain to set up the apology that very little damage is done. The antecedent transgressions, ending in a claim of title, enter into the present trespass and make it a question whether the rightful owner or the trespasser shall hold possession. Here the rightful owner is the people of the United States, and the trespasser is Andrew Johnson. Therefore in the name of the people is he impeached.

This simple illustration opens the whole case. The mere technical violation of a statute or of the Constitution, without antecedents and without consequents, would not justify an impeachment. All of us can recall such, even in the administration of Abraham Lincoln, and I cannot doubt that, since this proceeding began, the Chief Justice violated the Constitution when he undertook to give a casting vote, not being a member of the Senate. But these were accidents, besides being innocuous. From a violation of the Constitution or of a statute, the law ordinarily infers evil intent, and where such a case is submitted to judgment, it throws upon the violator the burden of exculpation. He must show that his conduct was innocent; in other words, that it was without evil intent or claim of title. In the present cause we have a denial of evil intent, with a claim of title.

The question of intent thus raised by this offender cannot be considered narrowly. This is a trial of impeachment, and not a criminal case in a county court. It is a proceeding for expulsion from office on account of political offences, and not a suit at law. When the offender sets up good intentions, he challenges inquisition, according to the latitude of such a proceeding. The whole past is unrolled by himself, and he cannot prevent the Senate from seeing it. By a commanding rule of evidence it is all before us without any further proof. You cannot shut it out; you cannot refuse to look at it. And yet we have been seriously told that we must shut out from sight everything but the technical trespass. It only remains that, imitating the ostrich, we should thrust our heads in the sand, and, not seeing danger, foolishly imagine it does not exist. This may do at Nisi Prius; it will not do in the Senate.

To such extent has this ostrich pretension been carried, that we have been solemnly admonished at the bar, and the paradox has found voice in the Senate, that we must judge the acts of Andrew Johnson "as if committed by George Washington." Here is the paradox in its length and breadth. I deny it. I scout it. On the contrary, I say that we must judge all these acts as if committed by Andrew Johnson, and nobody else. In other words, we must see things as they are. As well insist that an act of guilt should be judged as the mistake of innocence. As well argue that the stab of the assassin should be treated as the cut of the surgeon.

To the Apology of Good Intentions, I oppose all that long unbroken series of transgressions, each with a voice to drown every pretext of innocence. I would not repeat what I have already said, but, in the presence of this apology, it is my duty to remind the Senate how the career of this offender is compounded of falsehood and usurpation; how, beginning with promises to make treason odious, he soon installed it in authority; how, from declared sympathy with Unionists, white and black, he changed to be their persecutor; how in him are continued the worst elements of slavery, an insensibility to right and a passion for power; how in this spirit he usurped great prerogatives which did not belong to him; how in the maintenance of this usurpation he stuck at nothing; how he violated law; how he abused the pardoning power; how he prostituted the appointing power; how he wielded the power of removal to maintain his tyranny; how he sacrificed the Freedmen's Bureau and lifted up the Whiskey Ring; how he patronized massacre and bloodshed, and gave a license to the Ku-Klux-Klan; how, in madness, he entered into conflict with Congress, contesting its rightful power over the reconstruction of the rebel States, and, when Congress would not succumb to his usurpation, how he thwarted and villified it, expectorating foul-mouthed utterances, which are a disgrace to human nature ; how he so far triumphed in his wickedness that in nine States no Union man is safe and no murderer of a Union man can be punished ; and, lastly, for time fails, though not the long list of transgressions, how he conspired against the patriot Secretary of War, because he found in that adamantine character an obstacle to his revolutionary career. And now, in the face of this terrible and indisputable record, entering into and filling this impeachment, I hear a voice saying that we must judge the acts in question " as if committed by George Washington." The statement of this pretension is enough. I hand it over to the contempt it deserves.

THE MOOT-COURT APOLOGY.

Kindred to the Apology of Good Intentions, or, perhaps, a rib out of its side, is the Moot Court Apology, which pretends that the President, in removing Mr. Stanton, only wished to make a case for the Supreme Court, and thus submit to this tribunal the constitutionality of the tenure-of-office act.

By this pretension the Supreme Court is converted into a moot-court to sit in judgment on acts of Congress, and the President becomes what, in the time of Charles II, Roger North said good lawyers must be, a "put case." Even assuming *against the evidence* that such was his purpose, it is hard to treat it without reprobation. The Supreme Court is not the arbiter of acts of Congress. If this pretension ever found favor, it was from the partisans of slavery and State rights, who, assured of the sympathy of the court, sought in this way to complete an unjust triumph. The power claimed is tribunitial in character, being nothing less than a veto. Its nearest parallel in history is in the ancient Justitia of Arragon, which could set aside laws as unconstitutional. Our Constitution leaves no doubt as to the proper functions of the Supreme Court. It may hear and determine :" all cases in law and equity arising under the Constitution, the laws of the United States, and the treaties made under their authority ;" but this is all. Its business is to decide " cases ;" not to sit in judgment on acts of Congress and issue its tribunitial veto. If a " case" arises where a statute is said to clash with the Constitution, it must be decided as any other case of conflict of laws. But nothing within the just powers of the court can touch an act of Congress, *except incidentally,* and then its judgment is binding only on the parties. The incidental reason assigned, as, for instance, that a statute is unconstitutional, does not bind anybody, not even the parties or the court itself. Of course, this incidental reason cannot bind Congress.

On the evidence it is clear enough that the President had no honest purpose to make a case for the Supreme Court. He may have talked about it, but he was never in earnest. When asked by General Sherman "why the lawyers .could not make a case," he said in reply that " it was found impossible, or that a case could not be made up." And so at each stage we find him practically discarding the idea. He issues the order of removal. Mr. Stanton disobeys. Here was exactly his opportunity. Instead of making the case by commencing the proper process, he tells General Thomas to " go on and take possession of the office ;" and then, putting an end to this whole pretension of a case for the court, he proceeds to treat the latter in every respect, whether of law or fact, as Secretary, welcomes him to his cabinet, invites him to present the business of his department, and, so far from taking advantage of the opportunity he had professed to desire, denies its existence. How could he inquire by what authority Mr. Stanton assumed to hold the office of Secretary of War, when he denied, in fact, that he was holding it ?

Look a little further and you cannot fail to see the reason of this indifference. The old writ of *quo warranto* was the only process by which a case could be made; and this could be issued only at the suit of the Attorney General. Had the President made an order of removal, the Secretary would have been compelled to hold only by virtue of the law and the Constitution. In answer to the writ he would have pleaded this protection, and the court must have decided the validity of the plea. Meanwhile he would have remained in office. Had he left, the process would have failed, and there was no other process by which he could raise the question. The decision of the Supreme Court in *Wallace* vs. *Anderson* would prevent a resort to a *quo warranto* on his part, while the earlier case of *Marbury* vs. *Madison* would shut him out from a *mandamus*. The apologists have not suggested any other remedy. It is clear, therefore, that Mr. Stanton's possession of the office was a *sine qua non* to a case in the Supreme Court; and that this could be only by *quo warranto*. The local attorney employed by the President testifies that a judgment in such a case could not be reached within a year. This was enough to make it impracticable; for, if commenced, it would leave the hated Secretary at his post for the remainder of the presidential term. During the pendency of the proceeding Mr. Stanton would continue the legitimate possessor of the office. Therefore the commencement of a case would defeat the presidential passion for his instant removal. True to his passion, he removed the Secretary, well knowing that in this way he prevented a case for the court.

Against this conclusion, where all the testimony is harmonized, we have certain fruitless conversations with his cabinet, and an attempt to raise the question on a *habeas corpus* after the arrest of General Thomas. The conversations, whose exclusion has given a handle to the apologists, which they do not fail to use, only show that the President had made this question a subject of talk, and that, in the end, it was apparent that he could not make a case for the court so as to remove Mr. Stanton during his term, and as this was his darling object the whole idea was abandoned. The arrest of General Thomas seemed for a moment to furnish another chance; but it is enough to say of the futile attempt at that time, that it was not only after the removal of Mr. Stanton but after the impeachment had been voted by the•House.

Had the President been in earnest, it was very easy for him to make a case by proceeding against a simple postmaster; but this did not suit him. He was in earnest only to remove Mr. Stanton.

Nothing is clearer than that this Moot Court Apology is a wretched pretension and after-thought. It is the subterfuge of a criminal to cover up his crime—as if a surgeon had committed murder and then set up the apology that it was an experiment in science.

THE APOLOGY OF PREROGATIVE.

Then comes the Apology of Prerogative, being nothing less than the intolerable pretension that the President can sit in judgment on acts of Congress, and, in his discretion, refuse to execute them. This apology is in the nature of a claim of right. Let this be established, and instead of a government of laws, which is the glory of a republic, we have only the government of a single man. Here is the one-man power with a vengeance.

Of course, if the President can sit in judgment on the tenure-of-office act, and set it aside as unconstitutional, there is no act of Congress which he may not treat in the same way. He may set aside the whole succession of statutes for the government of the army : and his interview with General Emory attests his willingness to venture in that direction. In that spirit of oppression which seems to govern him, he may set aside the great statute for the establishment of civil rights without distinction of color. But why confine myself to instances? The whole statute-book will be subject to his prerogative. Vain is the requirement of the Constitution that "the President shall take care that the laws be faithfully executed." Vain is that other requirement, that a bill, approved by two-thirds of both houses over his veto, "shall become a law." His veto is perpetual; nor is it limited to any special enactment. It is as broad as the whole recorded legislation of the Republic. There is nothing which it cannot hurry into that maelstrom engulfing all.

The President considers the statute unconstitutional, say the apologists. A mistake in judgment on such a question is not an impeachable offence, add the apologists. To which I reply, that it is not for a mistake in judgment but for usurpation in undertaking to exercise his judgment at all on such a question that he is impeached; in other words, he is impeached for undertaking to set aside a statute. Whether the statute is constitutional or not is immaterial in this view. The President, after the statute has become a law, is not the person to decide.

Ingenuity seeks to perplex the question by putting impossible cases. For instance, suppose Congress should have lost its wits, so far as to enact, in direct terms, that the President should not be Commander-in-chief of the army and navy, or that he should not have the power to grant pardons; and suppose still further, that Congress, in defiance of the positive text of the Constitution, should undertake to create "titles of nobility," must not the President treat such enactments as unconstitutional? Of course he must; but such instances do not help the prerogative now claimed. Every such enactment would be *on its face unconstitutional*. It would be an act of unreasoning madness, which the President, as well as the courts, must disregard as if it were plain nonsense. Its unconstitutionality would be like an axiom, not to be questioned. No argument or authority would be needed. It proves itself. Nor would the duty of disobedience be less obligatory, even if the enactment had been sanctioned by the Supreme Court; and it is not more violent for me to suppose it sanctioned by the Supreme Court, than for the apologists to suppose it sanctioned by Congress. The enactment would be a self-evident monstrosity, and therefore must be disobeyed as much as if one of the ten commandments were reversed, so that it should read, "Thou shalt kill." Such extreme cases serve no good purpose. The Constitution is the supreme law of the land, and the people will not allow its axiomatic requirements to be set aside. An illustration outside the limits of reason is of no value.

In the cases supposed, the unconstitutionality of the enactment is axiomatic, excluding opinion or argument. It is a matter of fact and not a matter of opinion. When the case is one on which there are two sides or two different views, it is then within the domain of argument. It is in no sense axiomatic. It is no longer a matter of fact but a matter of opinion. When submitted to the Supreme Court it is for their "opinion." Without occupying time with refinements on this head, I content myself with asserting that the judgment of the court must be a matter of opinion. One of the apologists has asserted that such a judgment is a matter of fact, and, generally, that the constitutionality of a statute is a matter of fact. I assert the contrary. When a bench of judges stands five to four, shall we say that the majority declare a fact and the minority declare an opinion?

Assuming, then, what I think cannot be denied, that the constitutionality of a statute is a matter of opinion, the question occurs, what opinion shall be regarded for the time as decisive. Clearly the opinion of Congress must control all executive officers, from the lowest to the President. According to a venerable maxim of jurisprudence, all public acts are presumed to be correct; *omnia rite presumuntur*. A statute must be presumed constitutional, unless on its face the contrary; and no decision of any court is required in its favor. It is the law of the land, and must be obeyed as such. The maxim which presumes constitutionality is just as binding as the analogous maxim of the criminal law, which presumes innocence. The President reversing all this has presumed the statute unconstitutional, and acted accordingly. In the name of prerogative he has set it aside.

The apologists have been driven to invoke the authority of President Jackson, who asserted for himself the power to judge the constitutionality of an act of Congress, which in the course of legislation required his approval, although the question involved had been already adjudged by the Supreme Court. And he was clearly right. The court itself would not be bound by its adjudication. How could it constrain another branch of the government? But Andrew Jackson never put forth the pretension that it was within his prerogative to nullify a statute which had been passed over his veto in the way prescribed by the Constitution. He was courageous, but there was no such unconstitutional audacity in his life.

The apologists have also summoned to their aid those great instances where conscientious citizens have refused obedience to unjust laws. Such was the case of Hampden, who set an example for all time in refusing to pay ship money. Such also was the case of many in our own country who spurned the fugitive slave bill. These exalted characters, on their conscience, refused to obey the law and suffered accordingly. The early Christians were required by imperial mandate to strew grain on the altar of Jove. Though good citizens, they preferred to be martyrs. Such a refusal can be no apology for a President, who, in the name of prerogative breaks the great oath which he has sworn to see that the laws are faithfully executed. Rather do these instances, in their moral grandeur, rebuke the offender.

Here I turn from this Apology of Prerogative, regretting that I cannot say more to unfold its destructive character. If anything could aggravate the transgressions of Andrew Johnson, stretching in long line from the beginning of his administration, it would be the claim of right which he sets up. Under such a claim the slenderest violation of law becomes a high crime and misdemeanor, to be pursued and judged by an indignant people. The supremacy of the laws must be preserved or the liberties of all will suffer.

SWARM OF TECHNICALITIES AND QUIBBLES

I now come upon that swarm of technicalities, devices, quirks, and quibbles, which, from the beginning, have infested this great proceeding. It is hard to speak of such things without giving utterance to a contempt not entirely parliamentary. To say that they are petty and miserable is not enough. To say that they are utterly unworthy of this historic occasion is to treat them politely. They are nothing but parasitic insects, like "vermin gendered in a lion's mane;" and they are so nimble and numerous that to deal with them as they skip about, one must have the patience of the Italian peasant, who catches and kills, one by one, the diminutive animals that infest his person. The public has not forgotten the exhibition of "industrious fleas." The Senate has witnessed the kindred exhibition of "industrious quibbles."

I can give specimens only, and out of many I take one which can never be forgotten. It will be found in the Opinion of the senator from West Virginia, (Mr. Van Winkle,) which, from beginning to end, treats this impeachment as if it were a prosecution for sheep-stealing in the police court of Wheeling, and brings to the defence all the unhesitating resources of a well-trained criminal lawyer. This famous Opinion, which is without a parallel in the annals of jurisprudence, must always be admired as the marvel of technicality in a proceeding where technicality should not intrude. It stands by itself, solitary in its originality. Others have been technical also, but the senator from West Virginia is nothing else. Travelling from law point to law point, or rather seeing law point after law point skip before him, at last he lights upon one of the largest dimensions, and this he boldly seizes and presents to the Senate.

According to him there is no allegation in the articles, that the order for the removal of Mr. Stanton was actually delivered to him, and, this being so, the senator declares that "if there is evidence of a delivery to be found in the proceedings it cannot be applied to this article, in which there is no charge or averment." And this is gravely uttered on this transcendent occasion, when an indignant people has risen to demand judgment of a criminal ruler. The article alleges that the order was "unlawfully issued," and nobody doubts that its delivery was proved ; but this is not enough, according to this senator. I challenge history for another instance of equal absurdity in legal pretension. The case which approaches it the closest is the famous extravagance of the Crown lawyer in the British Parliament, who, in reply to the argument of our fathers, that they could not be taxed without representation, bravely insisted that they were represented, and sustained himself by saying that, under the colonial charters, the lands were held "in common socage as of the borough of Greenwich in Kent," and, as Greenwich was represented in Parliament, therefore the colonies were represented there. The pretension was perfect in form, but essentially absurd. The senator from West Virginia has outdone even this climax of technicality. Other generations, as they read this great trial, with its accumulation of transgressions ending in the removal of Mr. Stanton, will note with wonder that a principal reason assigned for the verdict of not guilty was that there was no allegation in the articles, that the order for the removal was actually received by Mr. Stanton, although there was a distinct allegation that it was "unlawfully issued," and, in point of fact, it was in evidence that the order was received by him, and no human being, not even the technical senator, imagined that it was not.

There is another invention, which has in its support some of the ablest of the apologists, like the senator from Iowa, (Mr. Grimes,) the senator from Maine, (Mr. Fessenden,) and the senator from Illinois, (Mr. Trumbull,) It is said that "as Mr. Stanton did not go out, therefore there was no removal ;" and therefore Andrew Johnson is not guilty. If, on an occasion like the present, the authority of names could change the unreal into the real, then this pretension might have weight. But it is impossible that anything so essentially frivolous should be recognized in this proceeding. Such are the shifts of a cause to be defended only by shifts. Clearly the offence of the President was in the order "unlawfully issued," and this was complete the moment it was delivered. So far as depended upon him, Mr. Stanton was removed. This was the way in which the country saw the transaction ; and this is the way in which it will be recorded by history.

But these same apologists, with curious inconsistency, when they come to consider the appointment of General Thomas, insist that there was a vacancy in point of law, called by the senator from Maine a *legal vacancy.* If there was such a vacancy, it was because there had been a removal in point of law. There is no escape from this consequence. If there was a removal in point of law, and there was no right to make it, the President was guilty of a misdemeanor in point of law and must take the consequences.

It would be unprofitable to follow these inventions further. From these know all. In the face of presidential pretensions, inconsistent with constitutional liberty, the apologists have contributed their efforts to save the criminal by subtleties, which can secure his acquittal in form only, as by a flaw in an indictment, and they have done this, knowing that he will be left in power to assert his prerogative, and that his acquittal will be a new letter of license. Nothing which the skill of the lawyer could supply has been wanting. This learned profession has lent to the criminal all the arts in which it excels, giving all to him and forgetting the Republic. Every doubt, every scruple, every technicality, every subtlety, every quibble has been arrayed on his side, when, by every rule of reason and patriotism, all should have been arrayed on the side of our country. The Public Safety, which is the supreme law, is now imperilled. Are we not told by Blackstone that the law is always ready to catch at anything in favor of liberty ? But these apologists "catch at anything " to save a usurper. In the early days of the common law there were technicalities in abundance, but these were for the maintenance of justice. On such was founded that extensive *ac etiam* jurisdiction of the King's Bench, which gives occasion for the elegant commentator to remark that, however startling these may be at first to the student, "he will find them, upon further consideration, to be highly beneficent and useful." (*Blackstone's Com.*, vol. III, p. 43.) But these generous fictions for the sake of justice must not be confounded with the devices by which justice is defeated.

The trick of the apologists has been this: by the stringent application of technical rules to shut out all except the offences charged in the articles, and then, when stress was laid upon these offences, to cry out that at most they were only technical, and too trifling for impeachment. To satisfy lawyers the House weakly declined to act on the bloody transgressions of two years; but they sought to provide against the future. Like the Roman ambassadors, they traced a line about the offender, which he was not to pass except at his peril. This was the line of law. At last he passed this line, openly, knowingly, defiantly, and now, that he is arraigned for this plain offence, we are told that it is nothing, only a little technicality. One of the counsel at the bar, Mr. Groesbeck, in a speech which showed how much feeling and talent could be given to a wrong side, exclaimed:

It almost shocks me to think that the President of the United States is to be dragged out of office on these miserable little questions whether he could make an *ad interim* appointment for a single day.

Only by excluding the whole context and all its antecedents could the question be reduced to this trivial form; and yet, even thus reduced, it involved nothing less than the supremacy of the laws.

I know not how such a question can be called "trifling." Often a great cause is presented on a narrow issue. Thus it was when English liberty was argued on the claim of ship-money, which was a tax of a few shillings only. Behind this question, called trifling by the kingly apologists of that day, loftily stood the great cause of the People against Prerogative, being the same which is now pending before the Senate. That other cause, on which at a later day hung the destinies of this continent, was presented on a narrower issue still. There was a tax of threepence a pound on tea, which our fathers refused to pay. But behind this question, so trifling to the apologists of prerogative, as behind that of ship-money, stood loftily the same great cause. The first cost Charles I his head. The second cost George III his colonies. If such a question can be disparaged as of small moment, then have the martyred dead in all times suffered in vain; then was the costly blood lavished for the suppression of our rebellion an empty sacrifice.

Constantly we are admonished that we must confine ourselves to the articles. Senators express a pious horror at looking outside the articles, and insist upon directing attention to these only. Here the senator from Maine is very strong. It is the "specific offences charged" and these only that he can see. He will not look at anything else, although spread upon the record of the Senate, and filling the land with its accumulated horrors. Of course such a system of exclusion sacrifices justice, belittles this trial, and forgets that essential latitude of inquiry which belongs to a political proceeding, having for its object Expulsion from Office only and not punishment. It is easy by looking at an object through the wrong end of an opera glass to find it dwarfed, contracted, and solitary. This is not the way to look at nature; nor is it the way to look at Andrew Johnson. This great offender should be seen in the light of day; precisely as he is; nor more, nor less; with nothing dwarfed; with no limits to the vision, and with all the immense background of accumulated transgressions filling the horizon as far as the eye can reach. The sight might ache; but how else can justice be done? A senator who begins by turning these articles into an inverted opera glass, takes the first step towards a judgment of acquittal. Alas! that the words of Burke are not true, when, asserting the comprehensive character of impeachment, he denied that, under it, "they who have no hope in the justice of their cause can have any hope that by some subtleties of form, some mode of pleading, by something, in short, different from the merits of the case, they may prevail." (*Bond's Trial of Hastings, vol. 1, p.* 11.) The orator was right in thus indignantly dismissing all questions of pleading and all subtleties of form. This proceeding is of substance and not of form. It is on the merits only that it can be judged. Anything short of this is the sacrifice of justice.

Such is the case of this enormous criminal. Events belonging to history, enrolled in the records of the Senate, and familiar to the country, are deliberately shut out from view, while we are treated to legal niceties without end. The lawyers have made a painful record. Nothing ever occurred so much calculated to bring the profession into disrepute; for never before has been such a theatre where lawyers were the actors. Their peculiarities have been exhibited to the world. Here was a great question of justice appealing to the highest sentiments and involving the best interests of the country—one of the greatest questions of all time; but the lawyers, in their instincts for the dialectics of the profession, forgot that everlasting truth which cannot be forgotten with impunity. They started at once in full cry. A quibble is to a lawyer what Dr. Johnson says it was to Shakspeare : " He follows it at all adventures ; it is sure to lead him out of the way ; it has some malignant power over his mind, and its fascinations are irresistible. A quibble is the golden apple for which he will always turn aside from his career ; a quibble, poor and barren as it is, gives him such delight that he is content to purchase it by the sacrifice of reason, propriety, and truth." In this Shakspearian spirit our lawyers have acted. They have pursued their quibbles with the ardor of the great dramatist; and even now are chasing them through the Senate chamber.

Unhappily this is according to history, and our lawyers are not among the splendid exceptions. But there is a reward for those who stand firm. Who does not honor the exalted magistrate of France, the Chancellor L'Hospital, who set such an example of rectitude and perfect justice ? Who does not honor those lawyers of English history, through whose toils liberty was upheld ? There was Selden, so wise and learned ; Pym, so grand in statesmanship ; Somers, who did so much to establish the best securities of the constitution. Nor can I forget, at a later day, that greatest advocate, Erskine, who lent to the oppressed his wonderful eloquence ; nor Mackintosh and Brougham, who carried into the courts that enlarged intelligence and sympathetic nature which the profession of the law could not constrain. These are among the names that have already had their reward, above the artful crowd which in all times has come to the defence of prerogative. It is no new thing that we witness now. The lawyer in other days has been, as we know him, prone to the support of power and ready with his technical reasons. Whichever side he takes he finds reasons, plenty as pins. When free to choose and not hired, his argument is the reflection of himself. All that he says is his own image. He takes sides on a law point according to his sentiments. Cultured in the law, and with that aptitude which is sharpened by its contests, too easily he finds a legal reason for an illegal judgment. Next to an outright mercenary, give me a lawyer to betray a great cause. The forms of law lend themselves to the betrayal. It is impossible to forget that the worst pretensions of prerogative, no matter how collossal, have been shouldered by the lawyers. It was they who carried ship-money against the patriot exertions of Hampden ; and in our country it was they who held up slavery in all its terrible pretensions from beginning to end. What is sometimes called the legal mind of Massachusetts, my own honored State, bent before the technical reasoning which justified the unutterable atrocities of the fugitive slave bill, while the supreme court of the State adopted this crime from the bench. Alas ! that it should be so. When will lawyers and judges see that nothing short of justice can stand ?

3 Sumner

After this survey it is easy for me to declare how I shall vote. My duty will be to vote guilty on all the articles. If consistent with the rules of the Senate I should vote, "Guilty of all and infinitely more."

Not doubting that Mr. Stanton was protected by the tenure-of-office act, and that he was believed to be so by the President, it is clear to me that the charges in the first and second articles are sustained. These two articles go together. I have already said in the course of this Opinion that the appointment of General Thomas as Secretary of War *ad interim* was without authority of law, and under the circumstances a violation of the Constitution. Accordingly the third article is sustained.

Then come what are called the conspiracy articles. Here also I am clear. Plainly there was an agreement between the President and General Thomas to get possession of the War Department, and to prevent Mr. Stanton from continuing in office, and this embraced the control of the mails and property belonging to the department, all of which was contrary to the tenure-of-office act. Intimidation and threats were certainly used by one of the conspirators, and in the case of conspiracy the acts of one are the acts of all. The evidence that force was intended is considerable, and all this must be interpreted by the general character of the offender, his menacing speeches, and the long series of transgressions which preceded this conspiracy. I cannot doubt that the conspiracy was to obtain possession of the War Department, peaceably if possible, forcibly if necessary. As such it was a violation of law, worthy of the judgment of the Senate. This disposes of the fourth, fifth, sixth, and seventh articles.

The eighth article charges that General Thomas was appointed to get the control of the moneys appropriated for the military service and the Department of War. All this would be an incident to the control of the War Department. In getting the control of the latter he would be able to wield the former. The evidence applicable to the one is also applicable to the other.

The ninth article opens a different question. This charges a wicked purpose to corrupt General Emory and draw him from his military duty. Not much passed between the President and the General; but it was enough to show that the President was playing the part of Iago. There was a hypocritical profession of regard for the Constitution, while he was betraying it. Here again his past character explains his purpose, so as not to leave any reasonable doubt with regard to it.

Then come the scandalous speeches, proved as set forth in the articles, so that even the senator from Virginia [Mr. Van Winkle] must admit that the evidence and the pleading concur. Here is no question of form. To my mind this is one of the strongest articles. On this alone, without anything else, I should deem it my duty to vote for expulsion from office. A young lieutenant, at the bottom of the ladder, if guilty of such things, would be "cashiered" at once. A President, at the top of the ladder, with less excuse from the inexperience of early life, and with greater responsibility from the elevation he had reached, should be "cashiered" also; and this is the object of impeachment. No person capable of such speeches should be allowed to govern this country. It is absurd to tolerate the idea. Besides being degraded, the country cannot be safe in such hands. The speeches are a revelation of himself, not materially different from well-known incidents; but they serve to exhibit him in his true character. They show him to be unfit for the official trust he enjoys. They were the utterances of a drunken man; and yet it does not appear that he was drunk. Now it is according to the precedents of our history that a person disqualified by drunkenness shall be removed from office. This was the case of Pickering in 1804. But a sober man, whose conduct suggests drunkenness, is as bad at least as if he were drunk. Is he not worse? If without the explanation of drunkenness he made such harangues, it seems to me that his unfitness for office becomes more evident, inasmuch as his deplorable condition is natural and not abnormal. The drunken man has lucid intervals; but where is the assurance of a lucid interval for this perpetual offender? Derangement is with him the normal condition.

It is astonishing to find that these infamous utterances, where ribaldry vies with blasphemy, have received a coat of varnish from the senator from Maine, [Mr. Fessenden,] who pleads that they were not "official;" nor did they "violate the Constitution, or any provision of the common or statute law, either in letter or spirit." In presence of such apologies for revolting indecencies, it is hard to preserve a proper calmness. Were they not uttered? This is enough. The drunkenness of Andrew Johnson, when he took his oath as Vice-President, was not "official;" but who will say that it was not an impeachable offence? And who will say that these expectorations differ in vileness from that drunkenness? If they did not violate the Constitution or any provision of the common or statute law, as is apologetically alleged, I cannot doubt that they violated the spirit of all laws. And then we are further reminded by the apologist of that "freedom of speech" which is a constitutional right; and thus, in the name of a great right, we are to give a license to utterances that shock the moral sense, and are a scandal to human nature. Spirit of John Milton! who pleaded so grandly for this great liberty, but would not allow it to be confounded with license, speak now to save this republic from the shame of surrender to an insufferable pretension!

The eleventh article is the most comprehensive of all. In some respects it is an *omnium gatherum.* Here in one mass is what is contained in other articles, and something else beside. Here is an allegation of a speech by the President in which he denied that Congress was a Congress; and then, in pursuance of this denial, it is alleged that he attempted to prevent the execution of the tenure-of-office act; also of an important clause in the army appropriation act; and also of the reconstruction act; and then the evidence followed, sustaining completely the allegation. The speech was made as set forth. The attempt to prevent the execution of the tenure-of-office act, who can question? The attempt to corrupt General Emory is in evidence. The whole history of the country shows how earnest the President has been to arrest the reconstruction act, and generally the congressional scheme of reconstruction. The removal of Mr. Stanton was in order to be relieved of an impediment to his purpose. I accept this article in gross and in detail. It has been proved in all its parts.

CONCLUSION.

In the judgment which I now deliver I cannot hesitate. To my vision the path is clear as day. Never in history was there a great case more free from all just doubt. If Andrew Johnson is not guilty, then never was a political offender guilty before; and, if his acquittal is taken as a precedent, never can a political offender be found guilty again. The proofs are mountainous. Therefore, you are now determining whether impeachment shall continue a beneficent remedy in the Constitution, or be blotted out forever, and the country handed over to the terrible process of revolution as its sole protection. If the milder process cannot be made effective now, when will it ever be? Under what influences? On what proofs? You wait for something. What? Is it usurpation? You have it before you, open, plain, insolent. Is it the abuse of delegated power? That, too, you have in this offender, hardly less broad than the powers he has exercised. Is it the violation of law? For more than two years he has set your laws at defiance; and when Congress, by a special enactment, strove to constrain him, he broke forth in rebellion against this constitutional authority. Perhaps you ask still for something more. Is it a long catalogue of crime, where violence and corruption alternate, while loyal men are sacrificed and the rebellion is lifted to its feet? That also is here.

The apologists are prone to remind the Senate that they are acting under the obligation of an oath. So are the rest of us, even if we do not ostentatiously declare it. By this oath, which is the same for all, we are sworn to do "impartial justice." It is justice, and this justice must be impartial. There must be no false weights and no exclusion of proper weights. Therefore, I cannot allow the jargon of lawyers on mere questions of form to sway this judgment against justice. Nor can I consent to shut out from view that long list of transgressions explaining and coloring the final act of defiance. To do so is not to render impartial justice, but to depart from this golden rule. The oath we have taken is poorly kept if we forget the Public Safety in devices for the criminal. Above all else, now and forever, is that justice which "holds the scales of right with even hand." In this sacred name, and in the name also of country, that great charity embracing so many other charities, I now make this final protest against all questions of form at the expense of the Republic.

Something also has been said of the people, now watching our proceedings with patriotic solicitude, and it has been proclaimed that they are wrong to intrude their judgment. I do not think so. This is a political proceeding, which the people at this moment are as competent to decide as the Senate. They are the multitudinous jury, coming from no small vicinage, but from the whole country; for, on this impeachment, involving the Public Safety, the vicinage is the whole country. It is they who have sent us here, as their representatives, and in their name to consult for the common weal. In nothing can we escape their judgment, least of all on a question like that now before us. It is a mistake to suppose that the Senate only has heard the evidence. *The people have heard it also, day by day, as it was delivered, and have carefully considered the case on its merits, properly dismissing all apologetic subtleties.* It will be for them to review what has been done. They are above the Senate, and will "rejudge its justice." Thus it has been in other cases. The popular superstition, which long surrounded the Supreme Court, could not save this tribunal from condemnation, amounting sometimes to execration, when, by an odious judgment, it undertook to uphold slavery; and down to this day Congress has justly refused to place the bust of the Chief Justice, who pronounced this judgment, in the hall of that tribunal where he presided so long. His predecessors are all there in marble; no marble of Taney is there. The present trial, like that in the Supreme Court, is a battle with slavery. *Acquittal is another Dred Scott decision*, and another chapter in the Barbarism of Slavery. How can senators, who are discharging a political function only, expect that the voice of the people will be more tender for them than it was for a Chief Justice pronouncing judgment from the bench of the Supreme Court, in the exercise of judicial power? His fate we know. Nor learning, nor private virtues, nor venerable years, could save him from justice. In the great pillory of history he stands, and there he must stand forever.

The people cannot witness with indifference the abandonment of the great Secretary, who organized their armies against the rebellion and then organized victory. Following him gratefully through the trials of the war, they found new occasion for gratitude when he stood out alone against that wickedness which was lifted to power on the pistol of an assassin. During these latter days, while tyrannical prerogative invaded all, he has kept the bridge. When at a similar crisis of English history Hampden stood out against the power of the Crown, it is recorded by the contemporary historian, Clarendon, that "he became the argument of all tongues; every man inquiring who and what he was, that durst at his own charge support the liberty and property of the kingdom and rescue his country from being made a prey to the Court." Such things are also said with equal force of our Secretary. Nor is it forgotten that the Senate, by two solemn votes of more than two-thirds, has twice instructed him to stay at the War Department, the President to the contrary notwithstanding. The people will not easily understand on what principle of Constitution, law, or morals, the Senate can twice instruct the [Secretary to stay, and then, by another vote, deliberately surrender him a prey to presidential tyranny. Talk of a somersault; talk of self-stultification; are not both here? God save me from participation in this disastrous wrong, and may He temper it kindly to our afflicted country.

For myself, I cannot despair of the Republic. It is a life-boat, which wind and wave cannot sink; but it may suffer much and be beaten by storms. All this I clearly see before us, if you fail to displace an unfit commander, whose power is a peril and a shame.

Alas! for all the evil that must break upon the country, especially in the suffering south, as it goes forth that this bad man is confirmed in the prerogatives he has usurped.

Alas! for that peace and reconciliation, the longing of good men, now postponed.

Alas! for that security, so important to all, as the only foundation on which to build, politically or financially. This, too, is postponed. How can people found a government or plant or buy, unless they are first secure?

Alas! for the Republic, degraded as never before, while the Whiskey Ring holds its orgy of corruption, and the Ku-Klux-Klan holds its orgy of blood!

Alas! for the hearts of the people, bruised to unutterable sadness, as they witness a cruel tyranny installed once more!

Alas! for that race so long oppressed, but at last redeemed from bondage, now plunged back into another hell of torment.

Alas! for the fresh graves, which already begin to yawn, while violence, armed with your verdict, goes forth, like another Fury, and murder is quickened anew.

Alas! for the Unionists, white and black alike, who have trusted to our flag. You now offer them a sacrifice to those persecutors whose representative is before you for judgment. They are the last in my thoughts, as I pronounce that vote which is too feeble to save them from intolerable wrong and outrage. They are fellow-citizens of a common country, brethren of a common humanity, two commanding titles, both strong against the deed. I send them at this terrible moment the sympathy and fellowship of a heart that suffers with them. So just a cause cannot be lost. Meanwhile may they find in themselves, and in the goodness of an overruling Providence, that rescue and protection which the Senate refuses to give.

[In the course of this trial there was an important claim of power by the Chief Justice, as presiding officer of the Senate, on which at the time Mr. Sumner expressed his opinion to the Senate, when it withdrew for consultation. As this claim was calculated in certain contingencies to affect the course of proceedings, possibly the final judgment, and as it may hereafter be drawn into a precedent, Mr. Sumner has been unwilling to lose this opportunity of recording his reasons against it. Therefore, to his Opinion on the merits, he annexes this further Opinion on an incidental question in the proceedings.]

OPINION OF HON. CHARLES SUMNER, OF MASSACHUSETTS, ON THE QUESTION CAN THE CHIEF JUSTICE, PRESIDING IN THE SENATE, RULE OR VOTE?

In determining the relations of the Chief Justice to the trial of the President, we must look, first, to the Constitution ; for it is solely by virtue of the Constitution that this eminent magistrate is transported from his own natural field to another, where he is for the time an exotic. Of course, the Chief Justice in his own court is at home ; but it is equally clear that when he comes into the Senate he is a stranger. Though justly received with welcome and honor, he cannot expect membership or anything beyond those powers which are derived directly from the Constitution, by virtue of which he temporarily occupies the chair.

Repairing to our authoritative text we find the only applicable words to be these :

The Senate shall have the sole power to try all impeachments. When the President of the United States is tried, the Chief Justice shall *preside;* and no person shall be convicted without the concurrence of two-thirds of the members present.

This is all. The Chief Justice shall *preside* but this is subject to two limitations specifically declared. First, the trial is to be by the Senate *solely*, and nobody else ; thus carefully excluding the presiding officer from all participation, except so far as is implied in the power to *preside;* and secondly, judgment of conviction can be only by a vote of "two-thirds of the *members present*," thus again excluding the presiding officer, unless it is assumed that he is a member of the Senate.

On the face of this text it is difficult to find any ambiguity. Nobody questions that the Chief Justice must preside. Can anybody question that the trial must be by the Senate *solely*, and nobody else? To change this requirement is to fly in the face of the Constitution. Can anybody question that the judgment of conviction must be by the votes of "*members* present," and nobody else? Now, since the Chief Justice is not a "member" of the Senate, it is plain that he is positively excluded from any vote on the final question. It only remains that he should "preside." And here the question recurs as to the meaning of this familiar term.

The person who presides is simply, according to the language of our rules, "presiding officer," and this designation is the equivalent or synonym of speaker, and also of prolocutor, each of which signifies somebody who speaks for the house. It is not implied that he votes with the house, much less that he decides for the house, but only that he is the voice of the house—its *speaker.* What the house has to say it says through him; but, except as the organ of the house, he is silent, unless he be also a member, when he superadds to his powers as presiding officer the powers of a member also. From this brief statement it appears at once how limited his functions must be.

4 Sumner

Here I might stop; but, since this question has assumed an unexpected
importance, I am induced to go further. It will be easy to show that the
language of the Constitution, if seen in the light of English parliamentary history, must have an interpretation identical with its natural import.

Nothing is clearer than this. If language employed in the Constitution had
already, at the time of its formation, received a definite meaning, it must be
interpreted accordingly. Thus, when the Constitution secures the "trial by
jury," it secures that institution as defined by antecedent English law. So,
also, when it declares that the judicial power shall extend to "all cases in law
and equity" arising under the Constitution, it recognizes the distinction between
law and equity peculiar to English law. Courts of common law and courts of
equity are all implied in this language; and, since there is no further definition
of their powers, we must ascertain them in England. Cushing, in determining
the rules of proceeding in our American legislatures, says :

Such was the practice of the two houses of the British Parliament when our ancestors
emigrated; and such has continued to be and now is the practice in that body. (Cushing,
Lex Parliamentaria, sec. 302.)

This resource has been most persuasively presented by Mr. Wirt, in his
remarkable argument on the impeachment of Judge Peck, where he has vindicated and expounded the true rule of interpretation.

According to this eminent authority, what he calls " the English archetypes"
were the models for the framers of our Constitution. The courts were fashioned
after these "archetypes." They were instituted according to " English *originals*,
to which they were manifestly referred by the Constitution itself." (Trial of
Peck, p. 499.) Here again I quote the words of Mr. Wirt.

All this is precisely applicable to that part of the Constitution now under
consideration. In its essential features it was borrowed from England. There
is its original, its model, its archetype. Therefore, to England we go.

Not only to England must we go, but also to parliamentary law, as recognized
in England at the adoption of our Constitution. The powers of a presiding
officer, where not specifically declared, must be found in parliamentary law.
The very term *preside* is parliamentary. It belongs to the technicalities of this
branch of law as much as *indict* belongs to the technicalities of the common
law. In determining the signification of this term it will be of little avail to
show some local usage, or, perhaps, some decision of a court. The usage or
decision of a Parliament must be shown. Against this all vague speculation or
divination of reason is futile. I will not encumber this discussion by superfluous authorities. In now insisting that this question must be determined by
parliamentary law, I content myself with citing the often-cited words of Lord
Coke in his Fourth Institute :

And as every court of justice hath laws and customs for its direction, some by the common
law, some by the civil and canon laws and customs, so the high court of Parliament *suis
propriis legibus et consuetudinibus subsistit*; all weighty matters in any Parliament, moved
concerning the peers of the realm or lords or commons in Parliament assembled, *ought to be
determined, adjudged, and discussed by the court of Parliament*, and not by the civil law, nor
yet by the common laws of this realm, used in more inferior courts. (Coke, 4th Institute,
p. 15.)

Here is the true rule. It is to "the course of Parliament" that we must
resort. It is in " the course of Parliament" that we must find all the powers
of a presiding officer, and all that is implied in the authority *to preside.* "The
Chief Justice shall *preside.*" Such is the Constitution. Nothing is specified
with regard to his powers. Nothing is said. What was intended was left to
inference from the language employed, which must be interpreted according to
" the course of Parliament ;" precisely as what was intended by *trial by jury*
is ascertained from the " common law." In the latter case we go to the " common law," in the former case we go to the " course of Parliament." You may
as well turn away from the common law in the one as from the " course of Par-

liament" in the other. In determining the "course of Parliament" we may resort to the summary of text-writers, and, better still, to the authentic instances of history.

Something has been said in this discussion with regard to the example of Lord Erskine, who presided at the impeachment of Lord Melville. This was in 1806, during the short-lived ministry of Fox, when Erskine was chancellor. It is by a misapprehension that this instance is supposed to sustain the present assumption. When seen in its true light it will be found to be in harmony with what appears to be the general rule. Erskine had at the time two characters. He was lord chancellor, and in this capacity was presiding officer of the House of Lords, without the right to rule or vote or even to speak. Besides being chancellor he was also a member of the House of Lords, with all the rights of other members. It will be seen, as we advance in this inquiry, that, again and again, it has been practically decided, that, whatever may be the powers of a presiding officer, who is actually a member of the body, a presiding officer who is not a member cannot rule or vote or even speak. In making this statement now I anticipate the argument. I do it at this stage only to put aside the suggestion founded on the instance of Lord Chancellor Erskine.

I begin with the most familiar authority—I mean the eminent writer and judge, Sir William Blackstone. In his Commentaries, where will be found, in elegant form, the complete body of English law, you have this whole matter stated in a few suggestive words :

The speaker of the House of Lords, *if a lord of Parliament*, may give his opinion or argue any question in the House.

Of course, if not a lord of Parliament, he could not give his opinion or argue any question. This is in accordance with all the authorities and unbroken usage ; but it has peculiar value at this moment, because it is the text of Blackstone. This work was the guide-book of our fathers. It first appeared in 1765–'69, the very period when the controversy with the mother country was fervid ; and it is an unquestionable fact of history that it was read in the colonies with peculiar interest. Burke, in one of his masterly orations, portraying the character of our fathers, says that more than one-half of the first edition of Blackstone's Commentaries was bought by them. Nothing can be clearer than that they knew it well.

The framers of the Constitution had it before them constantly. It was their most familiar work. It was to them as Bowditch's Navigator is to the mariner in our day. They looked to it for guidance on the sea they were traversing. When they undertook to provide that the Chief Justice, who was not a member of the Senate, should preside at the impeachment of the President, they knew well that he could have no power " to give an opinion or argue any question in the House ;" for Blackstone had instructed them explicitly on this head. They knew that he was simply a presiding officer according to the immemorial usage of the upper House in England, *with such powers as belong to a presiding officer who is not a member of the house, and none other.*

The powers of the presiding officer of the House of Lords are illustrated by authority and precedents, all in harmony with the statement of Blackstone. Ordinarily the keeper of the great seal is the presiding officer ; but he can do little more than put the question, unless he is a member of the body. Any other person, as a chief justice, may be delegated by royal commission. According to the rules of the house, even if he is a peer, he cannot speak without quitting the woolsack, which is the chair, and going " to his own place as a peer." The right of speech belongs to him as a member, but he cannot exercise it without leaving his place as presiding officer. To this extent is he circumscribed.

A late writer on parliamentary law, whose work is a satisfactory guide, thus sententiously sums up the law and usage :

The position of the speaker of the House of Lords is somewhat anomalous, for though he is the president of a deliberative assembly, he is invested with no more authority than any other member; and *if not himself a member, his office is limited to the putting of questions and other formal proceedings.* (May. Parliamentiary Practice, p. 220, chap. 7.)

This statement is in obvious harmony with that of Blackstone, so that there is no difference between the writer who is our guide to-day, and the learned commentator who was the guide of our fathers.

Mr. May goes still further, and lets us know that it is only as a member of the house that the presiding officer can address it, *even on points of order.*

Upon points of order the speaker, *if a peer,* may address the house, but as his opinion is liable to be questioned, *like that of any other peer,* he does not often exercise the right. (P. 220.)

Thus, even if a peer—even if a member of the upper house—the presiding officer cannot rule a point of order nor address the house upon it, except as any other member; and what he says is open to question, like the utterance of any other member. Such is the conclusion of the most approved English authority.

American writers on parliamentary law concur with the English. Cushing, who has done so much to illustrate this whole subject, says of the presiding officer of the lords that "he is invested with no more authority for the preservation of order than any other member, and if not a member, his office is limited to the putting of questions and other formal proceedings; if he is a peer, he may address the house and participate in the debate as a member." He then says again, "if a peer he votes with the other members; if not, *he does not vote at all;*" and he adds, "*there is no casting vote in the lords.*" (§ 288.) This statement was made long after the adoption of the national Constitution, and anterior to the present controversy.

There are occasions when the lords have a presiding officer, called a lord high steward. This is on the trial of a peer, whether upon impeachment or indictment. Here again we find the same rule stated by Edmund Burke, in his masterly report to the House of Commons on the impeachment of Warren Hastings. These are his words:

Every peer present at the trial and every temporal peer hath a right to be present in every part of the proceeding, voteth upon every question of law and fact; and the question is carried by the major vote, the lord high steward himself voting merely as a peer and member of that court, in common with the rest of the peers, and in no other right. (Burke's Works, vol. 6, p. 512, Bohn's Edition.)

In another place the report, quoting the Commons' journal, says:

That the lord high steward was but as a speaker or chairman for the more orderly proceeding at the trial. (Ibid., p. 515.)

In our day there have been instances where the lord chancellor sat as presiding officer without being a peer. Brougham took his seat on the 22d November, 1830, before his patent as a peer had been made out, and during this interval his energies were suppressed while he was simply presiding officer and nothing else. The same was the case with that eminent lawyer, Sir Edward Sugden, who sat as presiding officer on the 4th of March, 1852, although he was still a commoner; and it was also the case with Sir Frederick Thesiger, who sat as presiding officer on the 1st March, 1858, although he was still a commoner. These instances attest practically the prevalence of the early rule down to our day. Even Brougham, who never shrank from speech or from the exercise of power, was constrained to bend to its exigency. He sat as lord chancellor, and in that character put the question; but this was all until he became a member of the house. Lord Campbell expressly records that, while his name appears in the entry of those present on the 22d November, 1830, as *Henricus Brougham, Cancellarius,* "he had no right to debate and vote till the following day," when the entry of his name and office appears as *Dominus Brougham et Vaux, Cancellarius.*

I pass from these examples of recent history and go back to the rule as known to our fathers at the adoption of the Constitution. On this head the evidence is complete. It will be found in the State Trials of England, in parliamentary history, and in the books of law, but it is nowhere better exhibited than in the

Lives of the Chancellors, by Lord Campbell, himself a member of the House of Lords and a chancellor, familliar with it historically and practically. He has stated the original rule, and in his work, which is as interesting as voluminous, has furnished constantly recurring illustrations of it. In the introduction to his Lives, where he describes the office of chancellor, Lord Campbell enunciates the rule, which I give in his own words :

Whether peer or commoner, the Chancellor is not, like the Speaker of the Commons, *moderator* of the proceedings of the house in which he seems to preside. He is not addressed in debate : he does not name the peer who is to be heard. *He is not appealed to as an authority on points of order*, and he may cheer the sentiments expressed by his colleagues in the ministry. (Campbell's Lives of Chancellors, vol. 1, p. 17.)

The existing rules of the Senate have added to these powers ; but such is the rule with regard to the presiding officer of the House of Lords, *even when a peer*. He is not appealed to on points of order. If a commoner, his power is still less.

If he be a commoner, notwithstanding a resolution of the House that he is to be proceeded against for any misconduct as if he were a peer, *he has neither vote nor deliberative voice, and he can only put the question, and communicate the resolutions of the House according to the directions he receives*. (Ibid.)

In the early period of English history the chancellors were often ecclesiastics, though generally commoners. Fortescue, Wolsey, and More were never peers. This also was the case with Sir Nicholas Bacon, the father of Lord Bacon, who held the seals under Queen Elizabeth for twenty years, and was the colleague in the cabinet of Burleigh. Lord Campbell thus remarks on his position as presiding officer of the House of Lords :

Not being a peer, he could not take a share in the Lords debates, but presiding as Speaker on the woolsack he exercised a considerable influence over their deliberations. (Ibid., vol. 2, p. 104.)

Then again we are told :

Being a commoner, he could neither act as Lord Steward nor sit upon the trial of the Duke of Norfolk, who was the first who suffered for favoring Mary's cause. (Ibid., p. 105.)

Thus early do we find an illustration of this rule, which constantly reappears as we travel down the annals of Parliament.

The successor of Sir Nicholas Bacon was Lord Chancellor Bromley; and here we find a record interesting to us at this moment. After presiding at the trial of Mary, Queen of Scots, the lord chancellor became ill and took to his bed. Under the circumstances Sir Edmund Anderson, *chief justice of the common pleas, was authorized by the Queen to act as a substitute for the chancellor*, and thus the chief justice became the presiding officer of the House of Lords to the close of the session without being a peer.

Then came Sir Christopher Hatton, the favorite of Queen Elizabeth, and so famous as the dancing chancellor, who presided in the House of Lords by virtue of his office, but never as a peer. He was followed by the exemplary Ellesmere, who was for many years chancellor without being a peer, but finished his career by adding to his title as presiding officer the functions of a member. The greatest of all in the list now followed. After much effort and solicitation Bacon becomes chancellor with a peerage ; but it is recorded in the Lords' journals that when he spoke he removed " from the woolsack to his seat as a peer," thus attesting that he had no voice as presiding officer. At last, when the corruptions of this remarkable character began to overshadow the land, *the chief justice of the King's Bench*, Sir James Ley, was designated by the King to act as Speaker of the House of Lords. Soon afterward Bacon fell. Meanwhile it is said that the chief justice had very creditably performed "the duties of Speaker of the House of Lords." (Campbell's Lives of Chancellors, vol. 2, p. 443.) In other words, according to the language of our Constitution, he had *presided* well.

Then came Coventry and Finch as lord keepers. As the latter absconded to avoid impeachment by the House of Commons Littleton, *chief justice of the common pleas*, " was placed on the woolsack as Speaker." At a later time he received the great seal as lord keeper. This promotion was followed by a peerage, at the prompting of no less a person than the Earl of Strafford, "who thought he might be more useful if permitted to take part in the proceedings of the House as a peer than if he could *only put the question as Speaker.*" (Ibid., vol. 2, p. 585.) Clarendon in his history says that, as a peer, he could have done Strafford "notable service." (History of the Rebellion, book 3, p. 104.) But the timid peer did not render the expected service.

Then came the period of civil war, when one great seal was with the King and another was with Parliament. Meanwhile the Earl of Manchester was appointed Speaker of the upper house, and as such took his place on the woolsack. As a peer he had all the privileges of a member of the house over which he presided. Charles II, during his exile, had appointed Hyde, afterward Earl of Clarendon, as chancellor; but the monarch was for the time without a court and without a Parliament. On the restoration in 1660 the chancellor at once entered upon all his duties, judicial and parliamentary; and it is recorded that, "though still a commoner, he took his place on the woolsack as Speaker by prescription." (Campbell's Lives, vol. 3, p. 187.) A year later the commoner was raised to the peerage, thus becoming more than presiding officer. During illness from the gout the place of the chancellor as presiding officer was sometimes supplied by Sir Orlando Bridgman, *chief justice of the common pleas*, who, on these occasions, was presiding officer, and nothing more. Lord Campbell says "he frequently sat as Speaker in the House of Lords"—(Ibid., 279)—which means that he *presided.*

On the disgrace of Lord Clarendon, the disposal of the great seal was the occasion of perplexity. The historian informs us that " after many doubts and conflicting plans among the King's male and female advisers it was put into the hands of a grave common-law judge," (ibid., p. 272,) being none other than *the chief justice of the common pleas*, who had already presided in the absence of Lord Clarendon; but he was never raised to the peerage. Here we have another explanation of the precise relation of such an official to the House. Lord Campbell expressly remarks that " never being created a peer, *his only duty in the House of Lords was to put the question*, and to address the two houses in explanation of the royal will on the assembling of Parliament." (Ibid., p. 281.) Here is the same recurring definition of the term *preside*.

For some time afterward there seems to have been little embarrassment. Nottingham, who did so much for equity; Shaftsbury, who did so little; Guilford, so famous through contemporary biography, and Jeffries, so justly infamous—successively heads of the law—were all peers. But at the revolution of 1688 there was an interregnum, which brought into relief the relations between the upper house and its presiding officer. Jeffries, on his flight, dropped the great seal in the Thames. King James had gone. There was, therefore, no presiding officer for the Lords. In order to supply this want, the Lords, at the meeting of the Convention Parliament, chose one of their own number, the Marquis of Halifax, as their Speaker, and, in the exercise of the power inherent in them, they continued to re-elect him day by day. During this period he was strictly President *pro tempore*. At last, Sir Robert Atkyns, chief baron of the exchequer, a commoner, took his seat upon the woolsack as Speaker, appointed by the Crown. Here, again, we learn that "serious inconvenience was experienced from the occupier of the woolsack *not being a member of the House.*" (Ibid., vol. 4, p. 53) At last, in 1693, the great seal was handed to Sir John Somers, lord keeper; and here we have another authentic illustration of the rule. Although the official head of the English law, and already exalted for his ability and varied knowledge, this great man, one of the saviors of constitutional liberty in England, was for some time merely presiding officer. The historian records that " while he remained a commoner he *presided* on the woolsack only as Speaker," (ibid., p. 118;) that he "had only to put the question, and took no part in debate." (Ibid., p. 122.) This is the more worthy of notice because Somers was recognized as a consummate orator. At last, according to the historian, " there was a strong desire that he should take part in the debates;" and the King, to enable him to do this, pressed his acceptance of a peerage, which, after some further delay, he did, and he was afterward known as Lord Somers. (Ibid., p. 125.)

In the vicissitudes of public life this great character was dismissed from office, and a successor was found in an inferior person, Sir Matthew Wright, who was created lord keeper without a peerage. For the five years of his official life it is recorded that he occupied the woolsack, "*merely putting the question, and having no influence over the proceedings.*" (Ibid., p. 245.) Thus he *presided.* Then came the polished Cowper, at first without a peerage, but after a short time created a member of the House. Here again the historian records that while he remained a commoner "*he took his place on the woolsack as Speaker, without a right to debate or vote.*" It appears that "not being permitted to share in the debates of the House of Lords, he amused himself by taking notes of the speeches on the opposite sides." (Ibid., pp. 304, 305.) Afterward, even when a peer, and as chancellor, *presiding* at the impeachment of Sacheverell, Lord Cowper did not interfere further than by saying, "Gentlemen of the House of Commons," or "Gentlemen, you that are counsel for the prisoner may proceed." (Ibid., p. 318.)

Harcourt followed Cowper as keeper of the great seal, but he was not immediately raised to the peerage. It is recorded that during one year he had "only to sit as Speaker." (Ibid., p. 456.) That is, he had only to *preside.* Afterwards, as a peer, he became a member of the body. He was succeeded as chancellor by the Earl of Macclesfield, with all the rights of membership.

Lord Macclesfield, being impeached of high crimes and misdemeanors as chancellor, Sir Peter King, *at the time chief justice of the common pleas, was made presiding officer of the upper house,* with only the limited powers belonging to a presiding officer, who is not a member of the body. Here the record is complete. Turn to the trial and you will see it all. It was he who gave directions to the managers, and also to the counsel ; who put the question, and afterward pronounced the sentence ; but he acted always as presiding officer, and nothing else. I do not perceive that he made any rulings during the progress of the trial. He was chief justice of the common pleas, acting as president *pro tempore.* The report describing the opening of the proceedings says that the articles of impeachment, with the answer and replication, were read " by direction of Lord Chief Justice King, speaker of the House of Lords." (Howell, State Trials, vol. 16, p. 768.) This instance furnishes another definition of the term *preside.*

All this is compendiously described by Lord Campbell, as follows :

Sir Peter, *not being a peer, of course had no deliberative voice,* but, during the trial, as the organ of the house of peers, he regulated the procedure without any special vote, intimating to the managers and to the counsel for the defendant when they were to speak and to adduce their evidence. After the verdict of guilty, he ordered the Black Rod to produce his prisoner at the bar ; and the speaker of the House of Commons having demanded judgment, he, in good taste, abstaining from making any comment, dryly, but solemnly and impressively pronounced the sentence which the house had agreed upon. (Campbell's Lives, vol. 4, p. 609.)

This proceeding was in 1725. At this time, Benjamin Franklin, the printer-boy, was actually in London. It is difficult to imagine that this precocious character, whose observation in public affairs was as remarkable as in philosophy, should have passed 18 months in London at this very period without noting this remarkable trial and the manner in which it was conducted. Thus, early in life he saw that a chief justice might *preside* at an impeachment without being a member of the House of Lords or exercising any of the powers which belong to membership.

Besides his eminence as a chief justice, King was the nephew of the great thinker who has exercised such influence on English and American opinion, John Locke. Shortly after *presiding* at the impeachment as chief justice he became chancellor, with a peerage.

He was followed in his high post by Talbot and Hardwicke, each with a peerage. Jumping the long period of their successful administrations, when the presiding officer was also a member of the upper ·house, I come to another instance where the position of the presiding officer became peculiarly apparent; and this, too, occurred when Benjamin Franklin was on his protracted visit to London as agent for the colonies. I refer to Sir Robert Henley, who became lord keeper in 1757, without a peerage. The King, George II, did not like him, and therefore, while placing him at the head of the law, declined to make him a member of the house over which he was to preside. At last, in 1760, the necessities of the public service constrained his elevation to the peerage, and soon afterward George III, who succeeded to the throne without the animosities of his grandfather, created him chancellor and Earl of Northington.

For four years Henley, while still a commoner, was presiding officer of the House of Lords. During this considerable period he was without a voice or vote. The historian remarks that "if there had been any debates he was precluded from taking part in them." (Campbell's Lives, vol. 4, p. 188.) And then, again, in another place, he pictures the defenceless condition of the unhappy magistrate with regard to his own decisions in the court below, when heard on appeal, as follows :

Lord Keeper Henley, till raised to the peerage, used to complain bitterly of being obliged to put the question for the reversal of his own decrees, without being permitted to say a word in support of them. (Ibid., vol. 1, p. 17, note.)

Lord Eldon, in his Anecdote Book, furnishes another statement of this case, as follows :

When Sir Robert Henley *presided* in the House of Lords as lord keeper, he could not enter into debate as a chancellor being a peer, does: and, therefore, when there was an appeal from his judgment in the court of chancery, and the law lords then in the house moved to reverse his judgments, he could not state the grounds of his opinions and support his decisions. (Twiss's Life of Eldon, vol. 1, p. 319.)

And thus for four years this commoner *presided* over the House of Lords.

A few months before Henley first took his place as presiding officer, Franklin arrived in London for the second time, and continued there, a busy observer, until after the judge was created a peer. Even if he had been ignorant of parliamentary usage, or had forgotten what passed at the trial of Lord Macclesfield, he could not have failed to note that the House of Lords had for its presiding officer an eminent judge, who, not being a member, could take no part in its proceedings beyond putting the question.

Afterward, in 1790, there was a different arrangement. Owing to a difficulty in finding a proper person as chancellor, the great seal was put in commission, and Lord Mansfield, chief justice of England, was persuaded to act as presiding officer of the upper house. Curiously enough, Franklin was again in England, on his third visit, and remained through the service of Lord Mansfield in this capacity. Thus this illustrious American, afterward a member of the convention that framed the National Constitution, had, at two different times, seen the House of Lords with a presiding officer who, not being a member of the body, could only put the question, and then again with another presiding officer, who, being a member of the body, could vote and speak, as well as put the question.

But Franklin was not the only member of the national convention to whom these precedents were known. One or more had been educated at the Temple in London. Others were accomplished lawyers, familiar with the courts of the mother country. I have already mentioned that Blackstone's Commentaries, where the general rule is clearly stated, was as well known in the colonies as in the mother country. Besides, our fathers were not ignorant of the history of England, which, down to the Declaration of Independence, had been their history. The English law was also theirs. Not a case in its books which did not belong to them as well as to the frequenters of Westminster Hall. The State Trials, involving principles of constitutional law, and embodying these very precedents, were all known. Hargrave's collection, in several folios, had already passed through at least four editions some time before the adoption of our National Constitution. I cannot err in supposing that all these were authoritative guides in our country at that time, and that the National Constitution was fashioned in all the various lights, historical and judicial, which they furnished.

The conclusion is irresistible, that when our fathers provided that on the trial of the President of the United States "the Chief Justice shall *preside*," they used the term "preside" in the sense it had already acquired in parliamentary law, and did not intend to attach to it any different signification; that they knew perfectly well the parliamentary distinction between a presiding officer a member of the house and a presiding officer not a member; that in constituting the Chief Justic presiding officer for a special temporary purpose they had in view similar instances in the mother country, when the lord keeper, chief justice, or other judicial personage had been appointed to "preside" over the House of Lords, of which he was not a member, as our Chief Justice is appointed to preside over the Senate, of which he is not a member; that they found in this constantly recurring example an apt precedent for their guidance; that they followed this precedent to all intents and purposes, using, with regard to the Chief Justice, the received parliamentary language, that he shall "preside," and nothing more; that, according to this precedent, they never intended to impart to the Chief Justice, president *pro tempore* of the Senate, any other powers than those of a presiding officer, not a member of the body; and that these powers, as exemplified in an unbroken series of instances extending over centuries, under different kings and through various administrations, were simply to put the question and to direct generally the conduct of business, without undertaking in any way, by voice or vote, to determine any question preliminary, interlocutory, or final.

In stating this conclusion I present simply the result of the authorities. It is not I who speak; it is the authorities. My own judgment may be imperfect; but here is a mass of testimony, concurring and cumulative, without a single exception, which cannot err.

Plainly and unmistakably the provision in our Constitution authorizing the Chief Justice to *preside* in the Senate, of which he is not a member, was modelled on the English original. This English original was, according to the language of Mr. Wirt, the "archetype" which our fathers followed. As such it was embodied in our Constitution as much as if the Constitution in its text expressly provided that the Chief Justice, when *presiding* in the Senate, had all the powers accorded by parliamentary usage to such a functionary when *presiding* in the upper house of Parliament, without being a member thereof. In saying that he shall "preside" the Constitution confers on the Chief Justice no powers of membership in the Senate, and by the well-defined term employed, limits him to those precise functions sanctioned at the time by immemorial usage.

Thus far I have considered this provision in the light of authorities already known and recognized at the adoption of the national Constitution. This is enough; for it is by these authorities that its meaning must be determined. You cannot reject these without setting at defiance a fixed rule of interpretation, and resorting instead to vague inference or mere imagination, quickened, perhaps, by your desires. Mere imagination and vague inference—quickened, perhaps, by your desires—are out of place when parliamentary law is beyond all question.

Pardon me if I protract this argument by an additional illustration derived from our own congressional history. This will be found under the parallel provision of the Constitution relating to the Vice-President, which, after much debate in another generation, received an authoritative interpretation. It is as follows: "The Vice-President of the United States shall be *President of the Senate*, but shall have no vote unless they be equally divided." In other words, the Vice-President, like the Chief Justice, shall *preside in the Senate*, but, unlike the Chief Justice, with a casting vote. His general powers are all implied in the provision that he shall *preside*.

No question has occurred with regard to the vote of the Vice-President, for this is expressly regulated by the Constitution. But the other powers of the Vice-President, when *presiding* in the Senate, are left to parliamentary law and express rules of the body. Some of the latter were settled at an early day. On looking at the rules of the Senate adopted at the beginning it will be found that, independent of his casting vote, nothing was originally recognized as belonging to a *presiding* Vice-President beyond his power to occupy the chair. All else was determined by the rules. For instance, senators, when speaking, are to address the Chair. This rule, which seems to us so superfluous, was adopted 16th April, 1789, early in the session of the first Congress, in order to change the existing parliamentary law, under which a member of the upper house of Parliament habitually addresses his associates, and never the Chair. Down to this day, in England, a peer, rising to speak, says, "My Lords," and never "My Lord Chancellor," although the latter *presides*. Another rule, adopted at the same date, has a similar origin. By parliamentary law, in the upper house of Parliament, when two members rise at the same time, the House, by their cry, indicate who shall speak. This was set aside by a positive rule of the Senate that in such a case "the president shall name the person to speak." The parliamentary law, that the presiding officer, whether a member or not a member, shall put the question, was re-enforced by an express rule that "all questions shall be put by the president of the Senate."

Although the rules originally provided that when a member is called to order "the president shall determine whether he is in order or not," they failed to declare by whom the call to order should be made. There was nothing conferring this power upon the presiding officer, while, by parliamentary law in the upper house of Parliament, no presiding officer, *as such*, could call to order, whatever he might do as a member. The powers of the presiding officer in the Senate were left in this uncertainty; but the small numbers of senators and the prevailing courtesy prevented trouble. At last, in the lapse of time, the numbers increased and the debates assumed a more animated character. Meanwhile, in 1825, Mr. Calhoun became Vice-President. This ingenious person, severely logical, and at the same time enjoying the confidence of the country to a rare degree, insisted that, as a presiding officer, he had no power but to carry into effect the rules adopted by the body, and that, therefore, in the absence of any rule on the subject, he was not empowered to call a senator to order for words spoken in debate. His conclusion was given as follows:

The chair had no power beyond the rules of the Senate. *It would stand in the light of a usurper were it to attempt to exercise such a power. It was too high a power for the Chair.* The Chair would never assume any power not vested in it; but would ever show firmness in exercising those powers that were vested in the Chair. (Congressional Debates, 1825-'26, p. 759.)

The question with regard to the powers of the Chair was transferred from the Senate chamber to the public press, where it was discussed with memorable ability. An article in the National Intelligencer, under the signature of Patrick Henry, attributed to John Quincy Adams, at the time President, assumed that the powers of the Vice-President, in calling to order, were not derived from the Senate, but that they came strictly from the Constitution itself, which authorizes him *to preside*, and that in their exercise the Vice-President was wholly independent of the Senate. To this assumption Mr. Calhoun replied in two articles, under the signature of Onslow, where he shows an ability not unworthy of the eminent parliamentarian whose name he for the time adopted. The point in issue was not unlike that now before us. It was insisted, on the one side, that certain powers were *inherent* in the Vice-President as presiding officer of the Senate, precisely as it is now insisted that certain powers are *inherent* in the Chief Justice when he becomes presiding officer of the Senate. Mr. Calhoun thus replied, in words applicable to the present occasion :

I affirm that, as a presiding officer, the Vice-President has no *inherent* power whatever, *unless that of doing what the Senate may prescribe by its rules be such a power.* There are, indeed, inherent powers, but they are in the *body* and not in the *officer*. He is a mere agent to exercise the will of the former. He can exercise no power which he does not hold by delegation, express or implied. (Calhoun's Life and Speeches, p. 17.)

Then again he says, in reply to an illustration that had been employed :

There is not the least *analogy* between the rights and duties of a judge and those of a presiding officer in a deliberative assembly. The analogy is altogether the other way. It is between the court and the House. (Ibid., p. 20.)

It would be difficult to answer the reasoning of Mr. Calhoun. Unless all the precedents, in unbroken series, are set aside, a presiding officer not a member of the Senate has no *inherent* powers except to occupy the chair and to put the question. All else must be derived from grant in the Constitution or in the rules of the body. In the absence of any such grant we must be contented to observe the mandates of the "*Lex Parliamentaria.*" The objections of Mr. Calhoun brought to light the feeble powers of our presiding officer, and a remedy was forthwith applied by an amendment of the rules, making it his duty to call to order. Thus to his general power as presiding officer was superadded, by express rule, a further power not existing by parliamentary law ; and such is the rule of the Senate at this day.

I turn away from this Vice-Presidential episode, contenting myself with reminding you how clearly it shows that, independent of the rules of the Senate, the presiding officer *as such* had small powers ; that he could do very little more than put the question and direct the Secretary ; and, in short, that our fathers, in the interpretation of his powers, had tacitly recognized the time-honored and prevailing usage of Parliament, which in itself is a commanding law. But a Chief Justice, when presiding in the Senate, is not less under this commanding law than the Vice-President.

Thus far I have confined myself to the parliamentary law governing the Upper House of Parliament and of Congress. Further illustration may be found in the position of the Speaker, whether in the House of Commons or the House of Representatives. Here there is one cardinal distinction to be noted at the outset: *The Speaker is always a member of the House,* in which respect he differs from the presiding officer of the upper house in either country. As a member he has a constituency which is represented through him ; and here is another difference. The presiding officer of the upper house has no constituency. Therefore his only duty is *to preside,* unless some other function be superadded by the constitution or the rules of the body.

All the authorities make the Speaker merely the organ of the House, except so far as his representative capacity is recognized. In the Commons he can vote only when the house is equally divided. In our House of Representatives his name is sometimes called, although there is no tie ; but in each case he votes in his representative capacity, and not as Speaker. In the time of Queen Elizabeth it was insisted that "because he was one out of our own number and *not a stranger,*" therefore he hath a voice." But Sir Walter Raleigh replied that " the speaker was foreclosed of his voice *by taking that place.*" (D'Ewes's Journals, 683, 684.) The latter opinion, which has been since overruled, attests the disposition at that early day to limit his powers.

Cushing, in his elaborate work, brings together numerous illustrations under this head Here is his own language containing the essence of all :

The presiding officer, though entitled on all occasions to be treated with the greatest attention and respect by the individual members, because the power and dignity and honor of the assembly are officially embodied in his person, *is yet but the servant of the House, to declare its will and to obey implicitly all its commands.* (Cushing's *Lex Parliamentaria,* sec. 294.)

The duties of a presiding officer are of such a nature, and require him to possess so entirely and exclusively the confidence of the assembly, that, with certain exceptions, which will presently be mentioned, he is not allowed to exercise any other functions than those which properly belong to his office ; *that is to say, he is excluded from submitting propositions to the assembly, from participating in its deliberations, and from voting.* (Ibid., section 300.)

At an early day an English Speaker vividly characterized his relations to the House when he describes himself as "one of themselves to be the mouth, and, indeed, the servant of all the rest." (Hansard's Parliamentary History, vol. 2, p. 535.) This character appears in the memorable incident when King Charles in his madness entered the Commons, and going directly to the Speaker asked for the five members he wished to arrest. Speaker Lenthall replied in ready words, which reveal the function of the presiding officer : "May it please your Majesty, I have neither eyes to see, nor tongue to speak, *in this place,* but as the House is pleased to direct me, whose servant I am *here.*" (Hatsell, vol. 2, p. 242.) This reply was as good in law as in patriotism Different words were employed by Sir William Scott, afterward Lord Stowell, when, in 1802, on moving the election of Mr. Speaker Abbott, he declared that a Speaker must add "to a jealous affection for the privileges of the House an awful sense of its duties." (Hansard's Parliamentary History, vol. 36, p. 915.) But the early Speaker and the great judge did not differ in substance. They both attest that the Speaker, when in the chair, is only the organ of the House and nothing more.

Passing from the Speaker to the Clerk, we shall find still another illustration showing that the word *preside,* under which the Chief Justice derives all his powers, has received an authoritative interpretation in the Rules of the House of Representatives, and the commentaries thereon. I cite from Barclay's Digest the following summary :

Under the authority contained in the manner and the usage of the House, the Clerk *presided* over its deliberations while there was no Speaker, but *simply put questions and where specially authorized preserved order, not, however, undertaking to decide questions of order.* (Barclay's Digest, p. 44.)

In another place, after stating that in several Congresses there was a failure to elect a Speaker for several days ; that in the twenty-sixth Congress there was a failure for eleven days ; that in the thirty-first Congress there was a failure for nearly a month ; that in the thirty-fourth and thirty-sixth Congresses, respectively, there was a failure for not less than two months, the author says :

During the three last-named periods, while the House was without a Speaker, the Clerk *presided* over its deliberations ; *not, however, exercising the functions of Speaker to the extent of deciding questions of order,* but, as in the case of other questions, putting them to the House for its decision. (Page 114.)

This limited power of the Clerk is thus described in a marginal note of the author—"Clerk *presides.*" The author then proceeds to say :

To relieve future houses of some of the difficulties which grew out of the very limited power of the Clerk as a *presiding officer,* the House of the thirty-sixth Congress adopted the present 146th and 147th rules, which provide that, pending the election of a Speaker, the Clerk shall preserve order and decorum, and shall decide all questions of order that may arise, subject to appeal to the House. (Page 114.)

From this impartial statement we have a *practical definition* of the word *preside.* It is difficult to see how it can have a different signification when it is said in the Constitution "the Chief Justice shall *preside.*" The word is the same in the two cases, and it must have substantially the same meaning, whether it concern a Clerk or a Chief Justice. Nobody ever supposed that a *presiding* Clerk could rule or vote. Can a *presiding* Chief Justice?

51

The claim of a *presiding* Chief Justice becomes still more questionable when it is considered how positively the Constitution declares that the Senate " shall have the *sole* power to try all impeachments," and, still further, that conviction can be only by " the concurrence of two-thirds of the *members present*." These two provisions accord powers to *the Senate solely.* If a *presiding* Chief Justice can rule or vote, the Senate has not " the sole power to try ;" for ruling and voting, even on interlocutory questions, may determine the *trial.* A vote to postpone, to withdraw, even to adjourn, might, under peculiar circumstances, exercise a decisive influence. *A vote for a protracted adjournment might defeat the trial.* Notoriously such votes are among the devices of parliamentary opposition. In doing anything like this a *presiding* Chief Justice makes himself a *trier*, and, if he votes on the final judgment, he makes himself *a member of the Senate;* but he cannot be either.

It is only a casting vote that thus far the *presiding* Chief Justice has assumed to give. But he has the same power to vote always as to vote when the Senate are equally divided. No such power in either case can be found in the Constitution or in parliamentary law. By the Constitution he *presides* and nothing more, while by parliamentary law there is no casting vote where the presiding officer is not a member of the body. Nor does there seem to be any difference between a casting vote on an interlocutory question and a casting vote on the final question. The first is determined by a majority, and the latter by two-thirds; but it has been decided in our country that " if the assembly on a division stands exactly one-third to two-thirds there is the occasion for the giving of a casting vote, because the presiding officer can then, by giving his vote, decide the question either way." (Cushing, Lex Parliamentaria, section 306.) This statement reveals still further how inconsistent is the claim of the *presiding* Chief Justice with the positive requirement of the Constitution.

I would not keep out of sight any consideration which seems in any quarter to throw light on this claim; and therefore I take time to mention an analogy which has been invoked. The exceptional provision in the Constitution, under which the Vice-President has a casting vote on ordinary occasions, is taken from its place in another clause and applied to the Chief Justice. It is gravely argued that the Chief Justice is a substitute for the Vice-President, and, as the latter, by express grant, has a casting vote on ordinary occasions, therefore the Chief Justice has such when presiding on an impeachment. To this argument there are two obvious objections : first, there is no language giving any casting vote to the Chief Justice, and in the absence of express grant, it is impossible to imply it in opposition to the prevailing rule of parliamentary law ; and, secondly, it is by no means clear that the Vice-President has a casting vote when called to preside on an impeachment. On ordinary occasions, in the business of the Senate, the grant is explicit; but it does not follow that this grant can be extended to embrace an impeachment, in face of the positive provisions of the Constitution, by which the power to *try* and *vote* are confined to *senators.* According to the undoubted rule of interpretation, *ut res magis valeat quam pereat*, the casting vote of the Vice-President must be subject to this curtailment. Therefore, if the Chief Justice is regarded as a substitute for the Vice-President, it will be only to find himself again within the limitations of the Constitution.

I cannot bring this survey to an end without an expression of deep regret that I find myself constrained to differ from the Chief Justice. In faithful fellowship for long years we have striven together for the establishment of liberty and equality as a fundamental law of this republic. I know his fidelity and revere his services, but not on this account can I hesitate the less when I find him claiming for himself in this chamber an important power which, in my judgment, is three times denied in the Constitution : first, when it is declared that the Senate alone shall *try* impeachments; secondly, when it is declared that members only shall convict; and, thirdly, when it is declared that the Chief Justice shall *preside*, and nothing more, thus conferring upon him those powers only which by parliamentary law belong to a presiding officer not a member of the body. In the face of such a claim, so entirely without example, and of such possible consequences, I cannot be silent. Reluctantly and painfully I offer this respectful protest.

There is a familiar saying of jurisprudence, that it is the part of a good judge to amplify his jurisdiction: *Boni judicis est ampliare jurisdictionem.* This maxim, borrowed from the horn-books, was originally established for the sake of justice and humanity, that they might not fail; but it has never been extended to other exercises of authority. On the contrary, all accepted maxims are against such assumption in other cases. Never has it been said that it is the part of a good presiding officer to amplify his power; and there is at least one obvious reason—a presiding officer is only an *agent*, acting always in the presence of his *principal.* Whatever may be the promptings of the present moment, such an amplification can find no sanction in the Constitution or in that parliamentary law from which there is no appeal.

Thus, which way soever we turn, whether to the Constitution or to parliamentary law, as illustrated in England or the United States, we are brought to conclude that the Chief Justice in the Senate chamber is not in any respect Chief Justice, but only presiding officer; that he has no judicial powers, or, in other words, powers *to try,* but only the powers of a presiding officer, not a member of the body. According to the injunction of the Constitution, he can *preside*—" the Chief Justice shall *preside;* " but this is all, unless other powers are superadded by the concession of the Senate, subject always to the constitutional limitation that the Senate alone can *try,* and, therefore, alone can rule or vote on questions which enter into the trial. The function of a presiding officer may be limited, but it must not be disparaged. For a succession of generations great men in the law, chancellors and chief justices, have not disdained to discharge it. Out of the long and famous list I mention one name of surpassing authority. Somers, the illustrious defender of constitutional liberty, unequalled in debate as in judgment, exercised this limited function without claiming other power. He was satisfied to *preside.* Such an example is not unworthy of us. If the present question could be determined by sentiments of personal regard, I should gladly say that our Chief Justice is needed to the Senate more than the Senate is needed to him. But the Constitution, which has regulated the duties of all, leaves to us no alternative. We are the Senate; he is the presiding officer; although, whether in the court-room or the Senate chamber, he is always the most exalted servant of the law. This character he cannot lose by any change of seat. As such he lends to this historic occasion the dignity of his presence and the authority of his example. Sitting in that chair, he can do much to smooth the course of business, and to fill the chamber with the spirit of justice. Under the rules of the Senate he can become its organ, but nothing more.